Flea Market STYLE

EMILY CHALMERS

with words by Ali Hanan

photography by
DEBI TRELOAR

RYLAND PETERS & SMALL
LONDON • NEW YORK

First published in 2005.
This revised edition published
in 2018 by
Ryland Peters & Small
20–21 Jockey's Fields
London WC1R 4BW
and
341 East 116th Street
New York, NY 10029
www.rylandpeters.com

ISBN 978-1-84975-927-4

A CIP record for this book is
available from the British Library.

10 9 8 7 6 5 4 3 2 1

Printed and bound in China.

SENIOR DESIGNER Paul Tilby
SENIOR EDITOR Henrietta Heald
LOCATION RESEARCH Emily Chalmers
and Emily Westlake
PRODUCTION Patricia Harrington
ART DIRECTOR Gabriella Le Grazie
PUBLISHING DIRECTOR Alison Starling

Contents

Introduction

Imagine. It's a Saturday morning. Rather than heading to the high street or driving to a shopping mall, you have strolled to a local street market. Each stall brims with gems. In amongst the piles of bric-à-brac are vintage fabrics, polished silver flatware, fine bone-china teacups, and – look! – there's a diamond, a glossy chestnut leather club chair complete with its original soft velvet cushion.

Sigh. If only your wicker shopping bag were a hundred times larger and came with wheels and an engine. High-street buys pale beside second-hand pieces with colourful past lives. What's more, such pieces survive because they were built for years of service. Old-timers such as copper pots, heirloom linens, mahogany rolltop desks and cast-iron kettles have done their time and lived to tell the tale. Some pieces were created with an artistry increasingly rare and precious in an age of mass-production. The errant line on a hand-painted roll of wallpaper or a thumbprint on a hand-made vase gives these pieces a spark of humanity.

Beautiful things never go out of style. Classics endure. And, if it's your lucky day, you may even bag a real gem, like an original Eames chair or a swooping Castiglioni 'Arco' lamp. Pieces like this retain – and even increase – their value.

Some preloved pieces will be welcomed as they are but others will need a little tender loving care or even urgent cosmetic surgery. Choose a piece if it has promise. If a sofa with good bone structure needs a facelift, for example, simply fashion a cover for it out of a vintage fabric. Other pieces can be resuscitated and reinvented. Dress up a cushion with an antique brooch or give a Plain Jane lampshade a gorgeous new gown made from old ribbons. Once you are a seasoned talent scout, you will be able to see a piece's potential and dream up a whole new career for it, like using a bench as a side table or a chipped teacup as a dainty vase.

Dip into the first part of the book, *Flea Market Finds*, to see what's on offer at antiques markets, second-hand stalls, car boot sales and online auctions. Whether your style is retro, minimalist, rock-'n'-roll or eclectic, you will see how to choose furniture, kitchenware, lighting and fabrics to suit it. *Putting It All Together* shows you how to transform your interior, room by room. The book ends with ideas on where to source finds. Apart from markets, items can also be found at car boot/ yard sales, reclamation yards and auctions, in skips/dumpsters and on internet sites.

Be inspired. Turn the pages and discover what kind of orphaned finds you can adopt and bring home to a new life. Shun the consumerism of the high street and the mall. Recycle and revive pieces with soul and style and you will be able to create a loved, lived-in space that you can really call home.

Flea Market FINDS

Old chairs, tables, beds, bookcases, desks, drawers, sofas, armchairs, stools and wardrobes come in all shapes, sizes and styles – and can often be picked up for a song. Choose pieces to suit your taste, or create your own eclectic look.

Furniture

A home furnished with second-hand pieces always seems more friendly, lived-in and loved than one furnished mostly with new items. Unlike their hot-off-the-shop-floor high-street counterparts, preloved items have a casual, congenial air. Some flea-market finds have their own quirks; others may need a bit of mending – but give any item a little tender loving care or a fresh twist and see it blossom into new life.

What's more, second-hand furniture comes in an enormous range of decorative styles. Timeless pieces, such as old leather sofas and refectory tables, have something in common with wardrobe staples such as faded denim jeans and little black dresses: they always look good. For urban loft dwellers, there are pieces to suit the raw aesthetic of industrial chic (think old dental chairs, office swivel seats, filing cabinets). For those who hanker after the soft, rustic look of country style, many markets have whole fields of furniture ripe for harvesting (think wicker storage baskets, wooden rocking chairs, farmhouse-style tables). And if your taste is retro, you will find a feast of vintage furniture, including wooden sideboards, kidney-shaped tables and

ABOVE Who would have imagined that this lovely lady in red would need to be rescued from a skip/ dumpster? She now looks stunning dressed with a vibrant scarf fashioned into a cushion cover.

OPPOSITE Many preloved pieces need a simple makeover. For example, a set of drawers that came from an office looks pretty in a coat of pink paint.

Think of yourself as a talent scout seeking supermodels. You will quickly learn how to spot a gorgeous piece at a hundred paces.

low-level vinyl sofas. Whatever your style, there will always be something to satisfy your magpie instinct.

While you are bound to find something to suit your taste, you will also find numerous classics at affordable prices. Buying brand-new high-quality pieces is very expensive, and if you buy inexpensive new furniture the choice is mainly restricted to flat-packed items, which tend to push a self-destruct button after only a few months of use. If you bone up on design classics, you might even unearth a coveted gem such as an original Verner Panton 'S' chair or a Charles and Ray Eames recliner. Such treasures will retain or even increase their value if kept in mint condition, so when it comes to reselling them you could be (literally) sitting on a small fortune.

When it comes to buying second-hand furniture, think of yourself as a talent scout searching for potential supermodels. You will quickly learn how to spot a good piece at a hundred paces. Start by checking for sound bone structure – a sturdy frame, springs and legs, and intact stuffing. If a piece of furniture is in fairly good shape but looks tired and battered, think cosmetic surgery. It is easy to give furniture a facelift with

THIS PAGE Let an old sofa step out in style in a new dress; this one has had its ageing white cover dyed a refreshing blue.

OPPOSITE, ABOVE Hallways are frequently no more than traffic routes, but with a hip find such as this retro chair, you won't want to just walk on by.

OPPOSITE, BELOW LEFT A luxurious red leather sofa has had its sassy looks softened by a floral cushion sewn from an old kitchen curtain.

OPPOSITE, BELOW RIGHT This 'Swan' chair by Danish designer Arne Jacobsen was discovered at a Copenhagen market.

THIS PAGE An antique, gilt-edged console found at London's Portobello market gives a modern space an air of luxury. Adorning its top is an oriental-style glass tree plucked from a car-boot sale and now used to display jewellery. The print above is a common, but classic, art find.

Some found objects have quirks; some need mending – but give any item a
little tender loving care or a fresh twist and watch it blossom into new life.

a coat of paint, a new slipcover or a little
artful customizing. Do try pieces of furniture
before you buy it, as looks can be deceptive
(you don't want a spring sticking into the
small of your back when you're reading the
Sunday papers, for example).

Seating is an essential element of virtually
every space in the home, especially the
living room. When it comes to armchairs
and sofas, look for signs of use such as shiny
patches on arms or saggy seating. Those
details show that the seat is comfortable
enough to have been sat on for hours in the
past. One thing that seems to appeal to all

tastes is the come-hither allure of a plump
leather sofa. Other fabric-covered pieces may
be found in great shape but with a dated
'dress', so to speak, and they can be
re-upholstered in a new or vintage fabric.
For instant results, drape a bedspread,
checked blanket or faux fur throw over the
sofa. Or add va-va-voom with cushions
fashioned from vintage fabrics and adorned
with brooches, ribbons or buttons.

While sofas and armchairs are at home in
living rooms, so too are pieces like chaises
longues and daybeds. Old chaise longues
often bring with them an air of elegance

ABOVE LEFT Bring old
pieces into rooms for which
they were not originally
intended. Repainted in a
crisp white, this chest of
drawers is at home in a
minimalist-style living room.

ABOVE A sideboard from
the 1960s is used for both
storage and display. The
'paint by numbers' picture
above it was inspired by a
vintage silk scarf pattern.

and grandeur. If quirky modern is your style, make a chaise longue more funky by re-covering it with a zebra print cover; if you're a classicist, complement its antique charm with embroidered silk cushions. These pieces can look seductive in a bedroom or decadent in a bathroom. A daybed is easy to make (simply shorten the legs of a small single bed) and is usually handier than a pull-out sofa for overnight guests. Create a backrest of multicoloured cushions for daytime use.

Another junk find that's often dismissed is the bench – think old church pews or school assembly benches. Often made from good-quality wood, a bench can double as a table or as overflow seating for dinner parties. To make it comfortable, simply fashion some squab cushions from vintage fabrics.

The choice of chairs is as endless as the way in which they can be used. Seek out old wrought-iron chairs, ex-café chairs, metal stools, rocking chairs and wicker chairs for every room, but also think laterally, bringing home retired 'working' chairs such as dentists' chairs, old cinema seats, massage therapists' chairs, bar stools, architects' chairs, laboratory stools and office chairs. Your finds may need a little paintwork here or a new cover there, but they will introduce into your home elements that are slightly eccentric and fabulously original.

You may find it hard to find a complete set of dining chairs, so cherry-pick individual chairs with a common theme (folding garden chairs, wooden café chairs or 1960s chairs) to create harmony – or go eclectic and create an array of mismatching chairs, softening hard edges and giving a sense of 'family' with a range of matching cushions.

When it comes to tables, aficionados can choose from second-hand office desks, old garden tables,

THIS PAGE A handsome cabinet with sliding doors offers generous storage for all sorts of recycled boxes housing odds and ends.

OPPOSITE, LEFT A piece of salvaged netting divides this living space into zones. The chair is an electric massage chair; originally clad in vinyl, it has been re-upholstered in floral fabric for a softer look.

OPPOSITE, RIGHT Outdoor pieces can work well indoors; this former wirework plant stand has been reinvented as storage for books and ornaments.

THIS PAGE AND OPPOSITE
Be inventive, like the owner of this house, who has jazzed up pieces of furniture with a coat of blackboard paint. She has chalked her son's name all over his chest of drawers and adorned the hall cupboard with poetry in a flowing, looping hand. These furniture sculptures are thrown into relief by a canvas of pale-grey walls.

THIS PAGE Markets and online auctions offer many storage pieces such as the chests below (left and right); customize them with brightly hued paints. A set of mirrors in various shapes (below left) does the same job as a single long mirror.

OPPOSITE Once used to store household linens, this old wardrobe now houses a collection of tableware. Beside it is a found sofa, which demonstrates how a chintzy, kitsch piece can work brilliantly in a simple, pared-down setting.

bedside tables and pine refectory tables. The list is endless. If you have enough space, look for one of the many farmhouse-style pine tables that turn up at antiques markets or online auctions; if you don't have much space, alternatives include tables with drop or extendable leaves to accommodate extra guests. Then there is always the ultimate junk-find table: a sanded door or a large piece of heavy glass mounted on a pair of reclaimed trestles – just cover it with a beautiful cloth to hide its haphazard look.

You are likely to come across many retro kidney tables or bent-chrome-and-glass 1970s tables that can serve as coffee tables. As for bedside tables, the choice depends on how inventive you are. Tables big enough for a couple of books, a reading light and a water jug are easily fashioned out of small wooden stools, old school desks or even folding butler's tray tables.

Wooden tea trolleys make equally useful kitchen storage. Alternatively, you can shorten the trolley's legs or remove the casters to make an instant side table or children's crafting table. Many former work tables such as office desks, architects' drawing boards and sewing tables can be converted into home-office desks.

Practical and efficient storage is an essential component of any home. Chests of drawers, side cabinets, wardrobes, bookcases, plate racks and cupboards – in all shapes and sizes and a huge range of styles – turn up regularly at car boots/ yard sales, markets and online auctions. All you need to do to update them is to sand them down and give them a fresh coat of paint (chalk paint is perfect as it does not require any priming), or paper the doors (or the interior) with vintage wallpaper. Or you could customize doors and drawers with funky new handles (fashion one out of old rope or thick ribbon, or use vintage door handles). Old tea chests, antique leather suitcases, toy chests, big wicker baskets, old laundry baskets and wine crates also create covetable storage.

An easy way to introduce pattern, colour and texture into an interior is with textiles. Markets, car boot/yard sales and online auction websites are a treasure trove of curtains, quilts, lace, shawls, tea towels and end-cuts of fabric bolts in a wide range of weights, qualities and patterns. Another solution is the clever use of junk-find wallpapers.

Pattern and Colour

OPPOSITE **A boldly striped pillow and throw have been used to update an old leather sofa, whose arms fold down to create a daybed. A patchwork of wallpaper samples adorns the wall behind.**

ABOVE RIGHT **Don't judge a chair by its cover! If you love the shape of a chair but not its garb, simply have it re-upholstered.**

It's amazing how easily something ordinary can become extraordinary thanks to the addition of pattern and colour from fabrics, wallpapers or paints. Imagine covering a plain wall with a patchwork of wallpaper samples. Or visualize a minimalist bedroom with a decorative wrought-iron bed covered in a smooth white bedcover and an old wardrobe in the corner. Adorn the bed with just one colourful cushion and somehow the whole room will be transformed. It is softer. It has a centre. That is the quiet power of pattern and colour.

When you use pattern, remember that a little bit goes a long way. Pattern draws the eye, becoming a focal point, so combine it with plenty of large, plain areas. If you want your chintzy sofa to be your living room's star piece, keep the backdrop simple. Conversely, if you have discovered a roll of graphically decorated 1970s wallpaper, ensure that the sofa in front of it is neutral.

Colour schemes usually work best when devised in one of three ways: either by using contrasting colours (for example, red teamed with blue, or turquoise with orange); by using complementary tones of the same colour (for example, khaki, sage and moss green, or cobalt blue, azure and sky blue); or by combining harmonious colours (for example, ruby red and orange, or dark chocolate and violet).

Ideas for decorative schemes have many sources. You could base your colour palette on a find such as a roll of vintage floral wallpaper, a red leather sofa or a beautiful orange vase, or you might prefer to search for accessories once you have chosen your favourite paint colour as a backdrop. A fresh green, for example, may prompt you to track down natural or naturally inspired objects to accompany it, such as a nut-brown leather sofa, a wooden-framed mirror or a large leafy plant in a terracotta pot.

Remember that light colours make small spaces appear bigger, while dark colours make walls feel closer. If you want to alter the way your space is perceived, apply these rules by bringing colour, pattern and texture into the floor and walls – your interior's largest canvases.

Second-hand wall-hangings and wallpaper are ideal for revitalizing your space. Unpopular in the 1990s – when white paint splashed its way over

INSET **Stack patterned fabric finds to create small areas of visual interest.**

THIS PAGE **Just as you might do with an outfit, you can crown your sofa or bed with a chic accessory. Here, a trio of cushions made from vintage scarves turn heads on a bed.**

THIS PAGE Soften the hard edges of wooden chairs with cushions. This foursome was created from various floral finds. Being fashioned from fabrics with a related colour palette makes them into a set.

LEFT This beautiful fabric length, used as a curtain to block draughts, is an artwork in itself. The heavy door, covered in blackboard paint, is softened with a white lace curtain.

RIGHT Held in place by pebbles from the sea shore, a floral scarf makes a translucent blind/shade.

Avoid visual mayhem by papering a single wall and painting the room's other walls in a neutral colour.

OPPOSITE Use finds to create screens and drapes that dare to be different. This striking patchwork of silk scarves, all loosely tacked together, offsets the hard-edged feel of a former warehouse. An old metal postal cabinet is home to piles of fabric finds, all waiting to be used.

countless interior walls – wallpaper is now making a comeback. With it comes colour, pattern and, in some cases, texture. Flea markets and online auction websites offer a range of vintage papers. Visual mayhem can be avoided by papering a single wall and painting the other walls a neutral shade Sometimes you won't find enough wallpaper to cover the whole wall. If this happens, look for a complementary paper and paper the wall in alternating stripes. Some patterns can be overpowering, but, if you are passionate about a particular design (or find a beautiful piece of wrapping paper), use it to jazz up smaller surface areas, such as storage boxes, files, wardrobe doors, bedheads and boxed-in bathtubs. Old hand-painted papers are sometimes masterpieces in their own right. Turn them

into display items by inserting a cutting into a big wooden frame or using them to cover a wrap-around canvas.

When it comes to floors, you will unearth a wealth of coverings at second-hand markets and car boot/yard sales. If you discover a beautiful piece, nothing will show it off quite like a white or pale wood floor. For patterned looks, search for Turkish kilims or Indian dhurries – or, if you find a carpet you like, simply cut off a piece to use as a rug. Heavy quilts can also work on the floor. Animal skins feel sensuously soft underfoot, so hunt down sheepskin, cowhide, goatskin, fake zebra prints and similar pieces.

Many vintage fabrics are exceptionally good quality, such as antique linen, classic cotton, thick woollen blankets and handmade lace. Textiles that survive years

ABOVE LEFT Sew squares of handmade antique lace onto plain cushions to give them depth and texture.

ABOVE RIGHT Thick woollen rugs make hard-wearing chair covers. This old army rug is tacked onto the chair in a big blanket stitch.

LEFT Old Welsh blankets cover a pair of armchairs. Out of the blanket remnants a companionable stuffed dog was born.

of use do so because they are sturdy and resilient, and most of them are made of natural fibres. Some pieces may be slightly threadbare, frayed or faded, but these old dames will inject Oa relaxed, lived-in feel to your home.

Like the most durable fabrics, certain prints stand the test of time, including polka dots, stripes (particularly red and white or blue and white stripes), florals, graphic patterns, gingham, animal prints, crochet squares and paisleys. Patterns from different eras can work well together (an Art Deco print and a 1950s print, for example, or a 1970s paisley print with a 1930s floral design) and look equally alluring with modern prints. As with paint, you can either mix similar patterns or bring together polka dots, stripes and graphics for a bold, audacious look. Remember to make the most of pattern with plain. Your eye will appreciate a jewel-like collection of cushions on a fresh, white sofa or a patchwork quilt crowned with white linen pillows.

When you are looking for second-hand fabrics, start with conventional sources, but don't forget that vintage clothing is also a treasure trove of textiles waiting to be rediscovered. Vintage dresses, particularly those with full skirts, offer lots of fabric to recycle. To create felt, buy a heap of old woollen jumpers and put them through a hot wash in the machine. You can easily fashion these into cushion covers or use them to create a winter-weight patchwork quilt.

Other pieces to look out for are pashminas, large scarves and oversized shawls, which – in the same way that you would casually throw one over your bare shoulders – you can drape over sofas and armchairs or sew into cushion covers.

Heavy quilts and animal hides, such as sheepskin, goatskin and cowhide, make wonderfully soft and sensuous floor coverings.

ABOVE Antique handmade tablecloths make delicate window covers, allowing light to filter through while repelling inquisitive eyes.

LEFT Dress up a chair with cushions made out of little black dresses. Former sequinned gowns give this black linen-covered chair instant glamour.

INSET To achieve a country feel, combine various types of traditional pattern, such as paisleys, florals, checks and stripes.

THIS PAGE You might not think that a polka-dot handkerchief, a geometric scarf, a crocheted rug and two floral cushions would go together, but this artful ensemble is a fine example of effective combining.

OPPOSITE Create your own patchwork quilt from old baby's clothes, vintage dresses, scarves, curtains – whatever you can find. Add a colourful valance made from a disused tablecloth or fabric roll secured by the weight of the mattress.

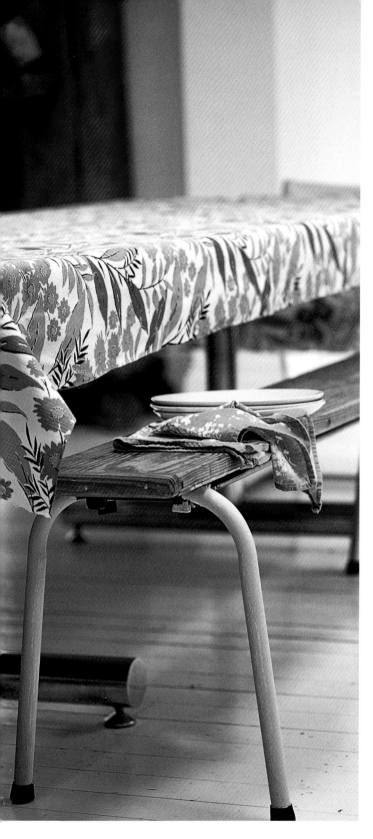

LEFT Hide battered tables under unusual tablecloths such as this one, created from the end of a fabric bolt. Antique linen sheets and Indian cotton bedspreads make good washable covers.

RIGHT Vintage tea towels made from robust old linens often surface at markets. Choose ones with funky retro designs.

Other clothes include silk scarves, which can also be used to make beguiling cushion covers or to adorn plain bedside tables. A black lace shawl could be converted into a window dressing (the light will diffuse through it beautifully). If you have no time for sewing, pay a visit to your local tailor and commission a piece. Cushion covers, for example, are a simple job and shouldn't cost much.

More conventional fabric finds, such as curtains, bedspreads and tablecloths, will easily find a use in your home. For example, if you possess a large sofa with a drab cover, a vintage bedspread or curtains swathed over the entire piece will hide a multitude of imperfections. Bedspreads, especially old Indian cotton ones, make funky tablecoths and generously large picnic blankets.

Curtains – such as the plush red velvet variety of curtain popular in the 1980s – can also be adapted to make covers for beds or cushions. Designed as an insulating material, luxurious velvet makes a snug winter bedcover. A patchwork quilt could become a striking living-room wall-hanging or a makeshift curtain in a child's room. Every fabric, conventional or otherwise, has endless possibilities.

One of the most rewarding fabrics to keep your eyes open for is antique linen. Once a treasured heirloom, old linen often turns up in markets and online. It is unbeatable for softness and resilience – consider, for example, freshly ironed linen sheets scented with lavender. If you find an old linen sheet, but parts of it are threadbare, cut it up into tea towels. Do as frugal housewives once did and cut down cotton sheets to make handkerchiefs and window-cleaning rags. Old linen tablecloths once came fringed with hand-stitched lace. When hung on a window, these make perfect blinds, letting in just enough light while simultaneously maintaining privacy. In addition to their obvious uses as soft furnishings, many fabrics can take on more off-beat roles. For an instant artwork, stretch a particularly beautiful piece over an old canvas – or, if you find a dress to die for, model it on a dressmaker's dummy for an instant artwork.

BELOW Introducing fabrics into an interior has an immediate softening effect, as demonstrated here by a brightly coloured blanket casually thrown over the arm of a sofa. Ethnic rugs of this type were indispensable features of 1960s style – as were flamboyant swirly patterns such as the one seen in the curtain fabric.

ABOVE Crochet throws lend a soft, homely feel to several rooms in the home. Sofas, armchairs, daybeds and beds all love curling up with a crochet rug.

Swathe a vintage bedspread or pair of old curtains over a drab sofa to conceal a multitude of imperfections. Bedspreads can also serve as funky tablecloths.

THIS PAGE From the tarnished silver cup to the antique scent bottle and the envelope fashioned from an old music score, these pieces share a similar palette and otherworldly feel so work well as a group.

INSET Create your own sparkling floral display out of crystal chandelier drops and artificial flowers made from antique fabric scraps stretched around pliable piping. Arrange with care in a sturdy vase to match.

Ceramics and glass are the jewels of your interior space. Just as a ruby pendant can transform a little black dress, so can a single red vase add vibrancy and a touch of drama to a slate-grey room.

Ceramics and Glass

Use ceramics and glass to add glamour and beauty to your home. Imagine, for example, a windowsill adorned with a string of sparkling perfume bottles or a table dressed with a necklace of Moroccan tea glasses with glowing tea lights inside. Allow yourself to be seduced by shapely bowls, elegant vases and candelabra, handsome earthenware pots, dainty glasses and pretty plates. There is a multitude of castaways out there just begging to be rescued and brought home.

Such beautiful vintage finds are very much in vogue. Open any interiors magazine and you'll see how desirable preloved glassware and ceramics have become. Pieces such as delicate bone-china teacups, pressed glass cake stands and futuristic, boldly coloured 1950s vases are selling like hot cakes at markets, antiques fairs and online and seem to be usurping their modern counterparts in many homes. This may be because vintage items introduce a bit of soul into clean-lined modern interiors – or because they retain an artistry that is lost in mass-produced pieces.

With decades of different styles to choose from you will find pieces to satisfy your taste. Go retro with chunky, funky 1950s pots, or classical with large Roman terracotta pots. Those with a penchant for global style can mix traditional pale blue-and-white Wedgwood plates (which can also be valuable) with aqua-blue glazed tagines from a Marrakech souk.

ABOVE Ceramic and glass vessels make colourful, containers for kitchen herbs.

RIGHT Unusual flowers bring a born-again quality to second-hand vases.

OPPOSITE, MAIN PICTURE This set of large, sculptural vases had a rather macabre past life as containers for graveyard flowers. Now packed with hydrangeas and reborn in a dining-room table display, they are full of life's joys.

OPPOSITE, INSET A Grecian urn-shaped vase is given a contemporary spin with a bouquet of sunny yellow roses.

Allow yourself to be seduced by stall after stall of shapely bowls, vases and candelabra, handsome earthenware pots, dainty glasses and pretty plates.

Fans of a simple, rustic look will revel in the assortment of floral vases or stripy ceramics. And if minimalism is your thing, rummage for Japanese tea sets and celadon rice bowls to adorn windowsills.

While many ceramic and glass vessels have their conventional uses, you can create unusual features with everyday items. Chinese vases, for example, double as beautiful storage pots, while long-necked vases work as candelabra, and dainty milk jugs make elegant desk tidies. Old glass jars serve as beautiful lanterns for tea lights, as do other vessels, particularly multi-coloured glass dessert bowls or blue-glass wine goblets. Extra large pieces, such as old Chinese vases or Arabic earthenware pots, can be transformed into umbrella stands.

Many ceramic or glass finds make original flower vases. Second-hand finds allow you to create startling, eye-catching looks with unusual pairings. Pop large-headed blooms into dainty mismatched teacups, for example, or gather a few long-stemmed delphiniums in an old wine decanter. You could adorn eggcups with individual carnation heads or arrange pink roses in Moroccan tea glasses.

Old milk jugs, kitchen jars, tea caddies, large mugs and teapots make unusual containers in which to grow parsley, sage, dill, basil and other culinary herbs on a sunny windowsill. Grow a fern in a ceramic chamber pot, or crown a low-level vase with a plume of long grasses. For plants that need plenty of watering, drill holes in the

OPPOSITE Display your glass jewels in a place where they can be properly admired. This collection of seconds and samples from a glassware factory adorn simple glass shelves. They have been placed in such a way as to catch the sun, so that a rainbow of light falls around a minimal room.

bottom of containers using a drill bit appropriate for the material. Put these planters on old saucers or large white dinner plates.

Ceramic tiles are junk must-haves. When new owners move into a house, they often strip out old pieces in the cause of modernization, and beautiful orphans can always be found at reclamation yards, online auctions and flea markets. These hand-made pieces possess a warmth and workmanship that distinguishes them from their mass-produced counterparts. Look out for old white and blue Delftware tiles, graphic 1970s-style tiles and traditional terracotta tiles. Being heat-resistant, these pieces can serve as useful coasters or trivets. If you can find enough tiles of the same style (or mix your finds with other pieces), use them to make kitchen splashbacks or to add visual interest to bathroom tiles.

When buying your pieces, keep in mind where they will live. Remember that one beautiful piece is often more eyecatching than a cluster of items. You will need to give your special piece enough space to breathe – place it in an alcove or against a white wall, for example; if it has star qualities, put it on show by shining a traditional brass picture light on it, or frame it with fairy lights.

If you want to group favourite finds together on window ledges, shelves and tabletops, buy pieces that vary in height, scale and size and use the

Cherish your collections. A wall of plates, a shelf of teapots or a window ledge of French milk jugs can make a beautiful focal point.

THIS PICTURE So kitsch –
and yet so beautiful. A
Japanese- style ceramic
sculpture of a blossoming
tree has been turned into a
convenient jewellery stand,
used to store – and to show
off – the owner's collection
of theatrical earrings.

ABOVE Invent new uses
for old vessels. No longer
needed as goblets, these
gilt-edged Danish twins
are now glamorous vases.

RIGHT Many glass
tumblers, goblets, bowls
and dishes can be reused
as candle-holders, as
exemplified by this petite,
pretty glass beaker.

LEFT Cracked and chipped
but by no means down
and out, a pair of perfume
bottles are born again
as ornaments. To attract
attention to their shapely
figures, they have been
adorned with jewels and
artificial butterflies.

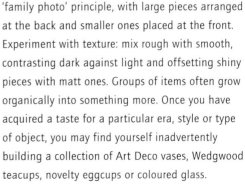

'family photo' principle, with large pieces arranged
at the back and smaller ones placed at the front.
Experiment with texture: mix rough with smooth,
contrasting dark against light and offsetting shiny
pieces with matt ones. Groups of items often grow
organically into something more. Once you have
acquired a taste for a particular era, style or type
of object, you may find yourself inadvertently
building a collection of Art Deco vases, Wedgwood
teacups, novelty eggcups or coloured glass.

THIS PAGE From the ceramic serving plates to the silver coffee pot, this beautiful collection of kitchenware should prompt you to hurry down to your local market and scour the stalls for classic items.

Gud velsigne vort Hjem.

RIGHT It is quite unusual to find a set of matching secondhand plates. Instead, you can assemble a dining set from an eclectic mixture of handsome plates.

Items such as oversized copper pots, dainty cut-glass cake stands, tiny gold salt bowls with fine spoons and silver flatware were once so cherished that pieces were passed down through the generations – and now they are turning up at markets.

Kitchenware

Once upon a time, in an era before ready meals, take-aways and online food delivery companies , cooking, serving and savouring food was a serious affair. The average time spent preparing evening meals in Britain was 60 minutes, while today it is a mere 13 minutes. Yet the rise of the TV dinner has proved a blessing for flea-market aficionados (and food lovers), who can now furnish their kitchens with beautiful, built-to-last cookware.

Many kitchen items have survived because they are robust, fashioned by artisans from good-quality materials. And there is something special about the warmth of a hand-painted bone-china coffee cup that leaves a mass-produced mug in the shade.

The errant line of a hand-beaten silver spoon has a more human quality than the regular, machined good looks of a piece straight off the factory production line. Second-hand tableware will provide endless topics for dinner-party conversation – after all, the discovery of each piece is often a story in itself. What's more, your finds may inspire culinary experimentation. If you like dinner parties with a twist, dine in with retro-style 1970s-style fondue sets and kitsch heart-shaped jelly moulds.

Continuing the second-hand theme, serve food on an array of mismatching dinner plates. If you can't find a complete second-hand dinner service, create your own from pieces that are in some way tied together by

ABOVE You can store rice, flour, sugar, pasta, biscuits and other groceries in vintage containers such as this assortment of kitsch, colourful retro tins.

THIS PAGE Once you start collecting orphaned pieces, you could soon find yourself with cupboards overflowing with treasures! This owner has stored items according to their culinary use – for example, oriental-style rice bowls and 1950s pastel-coloured tea cups. Other collections include retro-style espresso cups, casserole dishes, salad bowls, milk jugs and dining plates.

colour or pattern (all blue-and-white plates, for example). You will also find a wealth of flatware and kitchen tools at markets, car boots/yard sales and online auctions. Again, opt for pieces of a similar style, delving deep for once-sought-after bone-handled utensils, which are lovely to hold (but sadly not dishwasher-friendly) and three-pronged silver Georgian-style forks.

Serve your guests drinks from your found array of old tumblers, pint glasses and – for serious beer drinkers – tankards or Toby jugs. Scour markets for wine glasses with a similar look or shape, such as thin-stemmed red wine glasses with large bowls Saucer-shaped Champagne coupes reminiscent of *Breakfast at Tiffany's* sometimes put their pretty heads above the parapet at markets. These graceful

glasses went out of fashion because the flute shape was found to keep champagne bubbles fizzing for longer but if you believe that there is no reason not to quaff champagne quickly, invest in a set of dainty mismatching bowls. Hunt down other drinks accessories such as sherry decanters, ice buckets, ice tongs, wine coolers, waiter's corkscrews and bottle openers.

One reason why antique glasses and ceramics have come back into fashion is the return of social occasions based on food rituals, such as coffee mornings and afternoon tea parties. Coffee lovers will find plenty of retro coffee pots and percolators as well as examples of wooden coffee grinders and branded coffee-bean jars. Graphically decorated cups and saucers are always good retro buys.

ABOVE These eclectic finds were all cherry-picked over the years from the same big flea market in Brussels. The discerning owner has treasured pieces for their individual beauty, collecting shapes, colours and sizes from a range of different eras. Where possible, he has bought matching sets or hunted down groups of pieces with similar themes.

Antique glasses and ceramics have come
back into vogue with the return of coffee
mornings, tea parties and other events
based on food rituals.

RIGHT AND BELOW
People who love baking will feast on market offerings. From old measuring spoons to shaped cake tins/pans and cookie cutters, there is a wealth of once-loved culinary items available. Look for old wooden spoons, flour sifters, hand eggbeaters and ceramic mixing bowls.

OPPOSITE AND ABOVE
Many divorced teacups turn up as singles at markets. Matchmake them with saucer finds, pairing gilt-edged cups with similar saucers, for example. Alternatively, use teacups as tiny vases for single blooms or posies, or pop tea lights inside and use them as candle-holders.

Second-hand markets also serve up an array of tea paraphernalia – themed teapots, tea cosies, milk jugs, delicate sugar bowls, sugar-cube tongs, and strainers – but what they do best is teacups. Your chance of finding a complete set is very slim, so look for pieces that harmonize, such as an assortment of gold-rimmed china cups or dainty floral designs. To serve accompanying cakes, snap up a 1950s crystal cake stand or a tiered stand in silver and pair it with an ornate silver cake knife.

When it comes to cookware, you will find plenty of examples of large wooden spoons,

kettles, old copper pots, soup ladles, cookie cutters, ice-cream scoops, rolling pins, nutcrackers, old-fashioned egg beaters and, with luck, old scales complete with measuring weights – as well as other kitchen paraphernalia (floral tin flour sifters with handles, measuring spoons, pressure cookers, glass juicers).

When you have acquired such beautiful old things, you definitely don't want to hide them away in drawers, so display lovely serving dishes on racks or hang your old-style copper pots and pans from a rack with butchers' hooks.

Lighting seems like a detail – yet nothing can transform a room as radically. Turn a spotlight on an elegant vase or light a single naked flame in a dark room, and notice how the whole room is born again.

Lighting

Let's start with the practicalities. When you are out shopping, there are three kinds of household lights to look out for: general lighting (for overall illumination), task lighting (for performing particular, close-up tasks) and accent lighting (for aesthetics).

The only caveat to bear in mind when buying second-hand light fittings is to examine them for any signs of wear and tear such as exposed or loose wiring or bent socket pegs. If you have any doubts, get your lights checked and installed by a qualified electrician who can replace and rewire worn or damaged fittings.

For general lighting, keep your eyes open for a range of lights but take into account the shape, size and function of the room in question. Living rooms are for relaxation and conversation, so the lighting in them needs to be soft and convivial, never brash, bright

or clinical. If your living room is pint-sized, create optical illusions with lights – for example, wall sconces provide a wash of light across the walls, making them appear larger. Eschew low-hanging or large bold pendant lights in small rooms because these tend to draw the eye downwards, making ceilings seem lower.

General lighting should illuminate an entire room at the flick of a switch. It can take the form of wall sconces, standard lamps or pendant fittings, with or without shades. Wall scones from all eras turn up at flea markets and vintage stores and on the internet since these are often orphaned when people tear out old fittings when refurbishing their homes. There is always a good selection of utilitarian second-hand lamps at reclamation yards and markets, some of them discarded from former

ABOVE **An ornate glass-drop wall sconce with a duo of golden pleated shades creates a glamorous focal point by day, and, with the engraved mirror behind, provides a warm wash of light by night.**

OPPOSITE **Although this space is open plan, the two oriental-style pendant lights define the dining space. The artwork on the wall behind the table is an old piece of patterned linoleum hung from bulldog clips on nails.**

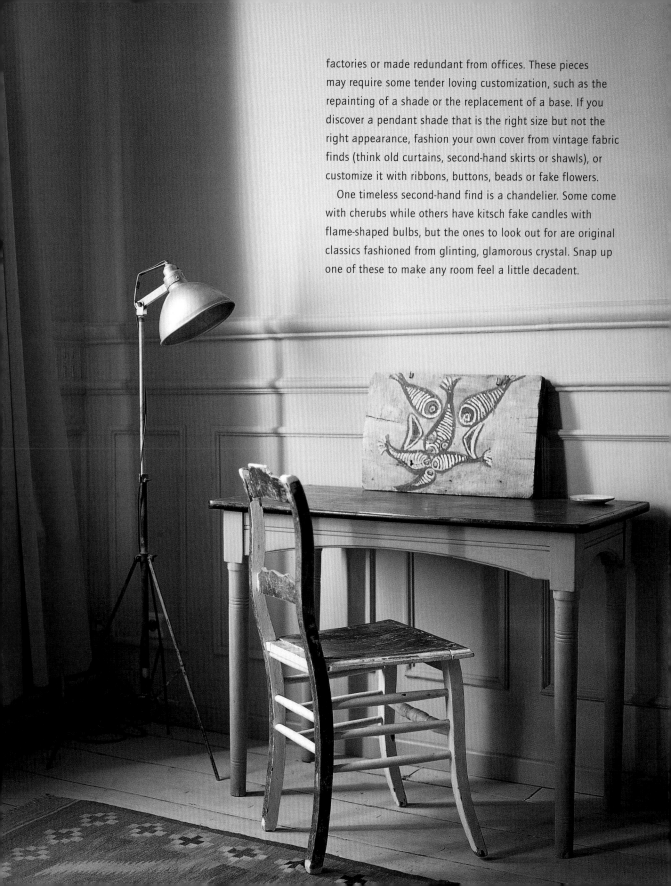

factories or made redundant from offices. These pieces may require some tender loving customization, such as the repainting of a shade or the replacement of a base. If you discover a pendant shade that is the right size but not the right appearance, fashion your own cover from vintage fabric finds (think old curtains, second-hand skirts or shawls), or customize it with ribbons, buttons, beads or fake flowers.

One timeless second-hand find is a chandelier. Some come with cherubs while others have kitsch fake candles with flame-shaped bulbs, but the ones to look out for are original classics fashioned from glinting, glamorous crystal. Snap up one of these to make any room feel a little decadent.

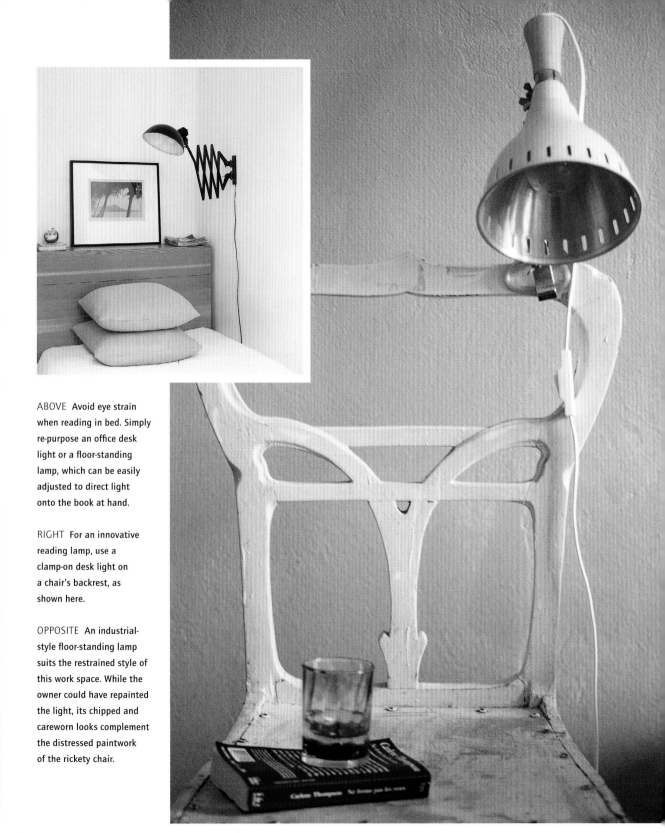

ABOVE Avoid eye strain when reading in bed. Simply re-purpose an office desk light or a floor-standing lamp, which can be easily adjusted to direct light onto the book at hand.

RIGHT For an innovative reading lamp, use a clamp-on desk light on a chair's backrest, as shown here.

OPPOSITE An industrial-style floor-standing lamp suits the restrained style of this work space. While the owner could have repainted the light, its chipped and careworn looks complement the distressed paintwork of the rickety chair.

LEFT Elegant glass drops dangling from metal fronds have been added to an industrial light to form a 'chandelier'. Alternative, similar drops might include colourful beads, ribbons or flower garlands.

BELOW This metal floral chandelier, of a type that came and went in a flicker during the 1950s, is a style of fitting that you are likely to see on your expeditions.

OPPOSITE, LEFT If your horizons are global, seek out light shades such as this intricate example found in a Moroccan market.

When it comes to task lighting, simply search for the right light for the job. For home offices, look out for articulated arm desk lamps such as the iconic Anglepoise, but ensure that the springs are operational. If they are too loose, you will end up with a floppy light; if they are too tight, you won't be able to adjust them. In living rooms, you will need reading sidelights (or angled wall sconces) and in bedrooms, bedside reading lights. Think laterally. An old desk lamp could easily make a bedside light. Table lamps are easy to create yourself. Introduce single items to each other to make beautiful marriages, such as an antique base and a funky 1950s shade, or a wooden base and a pleated pastel shade.

Accent or feature lighting highlights a little of what you fancy. Use it to draw attention to your most-loved possessions (use a downlighter, for example, to illuminate a loved painting). Alternatively, you can choose old lights

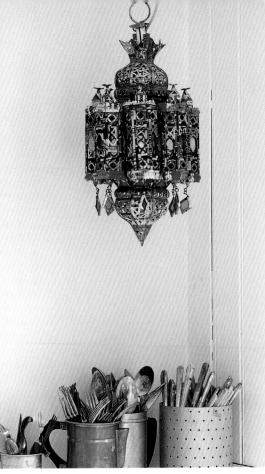

as pieces to admire for their own beauty
alone. If you love a chandelier's sense of
grandeur but don't want to wire it up, simply
hang it near a window so its faceted glass
droplets reflect the daylight. Other antique
lights simply look handsome, such as ornate
gas lights from yesteryear. For an air of
enchanted romance, look for strings of mini
lights. Some may require new bulbs or have
missing decorations, so customize them with
other finds, such as fake flowers or butterflies.
If you want to accent pieces of artwork, search
out traditional brass picture lights or frame a
painting with fairy lights.

Most of your creativity will go into lighting
your principal rooms, but keep the flea market
feeling alive in hallways and entrances and on

THIS PICTURE Just as
diamonds are a girl's best
friend, so chandeliers are a
room's best friend. If it is
too complicated to adapt
your chandelier to light a
modern room, use it as
decoration and hang it
where the natural light can
catch its sparkly drops.

staircases. It is easy to forget about these spaces, but funky lights help to make the most of what might otherwise be featureless passageways. Dot mismatching second-hand lamps up the staircase, for example, or run a length of fairy lights down a hallway to create eye-catching features. Of course, first impressions count, so ensure that your entranceway is well lit. This is the place to position one spectacular find, such as a customized chandelier or a big bold floor lamp with a graphic lampshade.

In conclusion, remember that the one style of light that never dates is candlelight. There is nothing more evocative than a naked flame. While you may not find many wax candles at second-hand markets or car boots/yard sales, you will find a glittery array of beautiful things to put them in – including old storm lanterns, oil lamplighters and grand silver heirloom candelabra. Many unconventional discoveries, such as vintage bottles, old vases, coloured tumblers and crystal dessert bowls, also make beautiful candle-holders.

ABOVE Pair lighting finds like this lovely blue base with a vintage lampshade. If a base is in good shape but the shade is past help, re-cover the shade's frame with a vintage fabric or wallpaper find.

RIGHT Fairy lights can create alluring shapes on walls. If a set of fairy lights have lost their decorations, you could fashion your own light garland from artificial butterflies or flowers.

Create a magical, mystical atmosphere at night by dotting lit candles around the house – in clusters in corners of the bathroom, in lines across the mantelpiece – and lighting a solitary flame in the bedroom.

LEFT A cherub balances on her hand a quartet of tapering candles, adding old-world glamour to a streamlined modern kitchen.

If there are certain items that you are passionate about, you may find yourself buying one more . . . and another. Gradually the hunt reaches fever-pitch and, before you know it, you have acquired a collection.

Collections and Display

OPPOSITE Collections are about whatever you want them to be. This mix of fossils, florets of coral, silver cups, candle-holders, trinkets and stuffed animals is the height of eclecticism.

ABOVE LEFT Exhibit your loved things for all to see (but not for little fingers to touch) in glass-fronted cabinets.

ABOVE RIGHT Tickle your fancy with fistfuls of coloured feathers in glass jars.

RIGHT A beautiful effigy of the Virgin Mary models a selection of necklaces, while a group of pictures and portraits behind the statue preserves memories.

Creating a collection is about bringing together beautiful things that you adore and indulging your whims. Whether you are in love with oil paintings, peacock feathers, army buttons, vintage clothes, 1930s vases, costume jewellery, faux flowers, pop memorabilia, tin soldiers or leather-bound poetry books, your hunt will take on a life of its own. Collecting brings out the hoarder in all of us.

Art collectors, for example, love antiques markets, where whole galleries of pictures await them. Choose pieces by genre – old oil paintings, for example – or by theme, such as landscapes, flower displays, portraits or dogs. Instead of just hanging pieces in conventional places, you could display them by grouping them on a wall or placing them on the floor propped against the walls along the length of a corridor. If you assemble a collection of pictures whose frames don't look right together, simply remove the frames and hang works from bulldog clips nailed to the wall or from pegs clipped to an old washing line. Otherwise, you could repaint the frames or replace them with beautiful alternatives, such as driftwood frames.

ABOVE LEFT AND RIGHT Markets are full of old oil paintings, but artists' palettes are rarer. Display artistic gems against a neutral backdrop

LEFT Hang pictures in groups for impact, but allow a bit of breathing space between them.

RIGHT Instead of using conventional frames, hang your photographs from the wall by bulldog clips attached to nails.

If you prefer photographic images, possible finds range from sepia-coloured portraits to black and white landscapes. If your own family portrait collection does not amount to much, you can adopt other people's photographs by buying old family photograph albums from markets. Vintage picture postcards are easy to source and can also be worth treasuring. To display such memorabilia, string them up with paperclips or safety pins, or tack them onto walls to make a collage.

If you can't find any pieces of art or sculptures you like, devise your own masterpiece. Take, for example, an empty gilt frame and hang it on a blank wall. Within its gilt-edged boundary, simply tack up pieces you love, such as pinned butterflies or fake corsages sprayed with glitter dust – or create still-lives from personal mementoes such as perfume bottles, once-loved toys, dried roses or tickets and banknotes acquired on foreign travels.

Mirrors, like paintings, look glamorous when grouped together, creating a feeling of light and space. Even a series of hand mirrors hung from a

wall look stunning. Choose pieces with different shapes or similar frames and use them to bring light into a dark corner like a stairwell or hallway.

Many fashionistas dedicate their flea-market legwork to finding beautiful vintage clothes as well as handbags, hats, shoes and boots. Instead of letting these pieces languish like wallflowers in wardrobes, put them on display. For example, you

LEFT When you follow your instincts and make impulse buys at different markets, you will often end up, over time, with various examples on the same theme, such as this pack of dog portraits.

ABOVE Other finds for walls might include old maps, like the one shown here, pieces of vintage wallpaper, antique fabrics stretched over canvases and linoleum offcuts.

BELOW AND RIGHT Use found objects to fashion your own still life on a sideboard. Here, some old coffee tins have been given a decorative makeover.

Many natural items turn up at markets – pieces of driftwood, coral, starfish, fossils or semi-precious stones such as amethysts.

could clothe a dressmaker's model in your favourite dress or simply hang much-loved pieces from coat hangers in open wardrobes or against wardrobe doors. Display shoes on a series of mini shelves or frame them in alcoves as if in a designer boutique. Handbags and hats can look striking when hung in groups from nails on the wall.

Other fashion accessories, such as feathers, fake corsages, brooches, ribbons, hairclips, lace and dress pins, can be used to transform cushions, rugs, and other home accessories. If you find some old brooches, for example, simply pin them onto one of your vintage cushions. Customize an old lampshade by tying a beautiful ribbon around it, or stick a series of feathers in its cap to give it instant panache. For a festive mood, create show-stopping garlands with a collection of artificial corsages strung together on a piece of coloured string or a long length of ribbon. You could also hang and

OPPOSITE, RIGHT **Display your vintage clothing collection on a dressmaker's model and change her dress weekly.**

THIS PAGE **Think about how to show off your finds to best visual advantage. For example, pieces of found wood could be arranged in groups like the spindly, attenuated ethnic figurines shown here, or made to stand to attention along a shelf (see inset).**

clip ribbons, artificial flowers and butterflies and bead necklaces to wire coat hangers (weave a couple together by the handles) to create a mobile for a children's bedroom. If you have found a chandelier with missing drops, such *objets trouvés* make gorgeous sparkly replacements.

Jewellery collections should never languish in a trinket box. Add glamour to walls, paintings, chairs and bedheads with strings of pearls, diamonds, opal pendants and shimmering silver chains. If you have some glittery glass beads, string them up on windows and mirrors or over lampshades so that they reflect the light, sending little coloured rays around the room.

Many natural items turn up at markets – pieces of driftwood, coral, starfish, fossils or semi-precious stones such as amethysts. Put such natural wonders where they can be appreciated or use them to

ABOVE LEFT AND RIGHT Instead of hiding your beautiful clothes, bags and shoes behind cupboard doors, put them where they can strut their stuff. Display them along a wall on coat-hangers hung from nails or picture hooks – or hang them from a metal kitchen rack. Recycle classic jackets and coats and keep your eyes peeled for good-quality, sturdy wooden coathangers.

OPPOSITE Store beautiful little things – feathers, buttons, ribbons, thread, theatrical jewellery, string, buttons, safety pins – in glass jars and use them to customize your outfits or your home's interior. In this room, heating pipes support an impromptu display of fake flowers, letters and toys. From the pipes hang butchers' hooks festooned with Christmas baubles and necklaces.

RIGHT Use capacious market bags as storage for your socks, lingerie and handkerchiefs.

LEFT From old postcards and photographs to mirrors and necklaces, the collection of intimate images on this wall makes for an original display.

THIS PICTURE AND RIGHT A collection of rosaries and crosses, some hanging from an ornate carved bedhead, adds an air of spirituality to a bedroom.

BELOW RIGHT AND OPPOSITE Walls make wonderful canvases for the display of market-found objects such as beads, shell necklaces, old postcards and hand-stitched lace. Other finds, such as dried flowers and autumn leaves, come from nature itself. Beautiful, fragile pieces like these allow you to create a 'found' artwork against a plain backdrop.

create original works of art. Fashion driftwood into a photograph or mirror frame or drill tiny holes in a smooth, organic-shaped piece to put your sticks of incense in.

Most market aficionados are inevitably drawn towards the second-hand book and magazine section since there will always be something there to covet. From dusty copies of Charles Dickens's *Oliver Twist* to ancient Mickey Mouse comics, you are likely to discover something to stimulate your imagination on virtually every subject.

If you collect old magazines, you can always tear out pages and use them to make picture collages to adorn your walls. Or, to enliven children's rooms, you could paste up pages from old comics to create original wallpaper that will absorb the little ones for hours. When it comes to displaying your literary finds,

LEFT AND ABOVE (TOP) Letters from shop fronts and printing blocks can make interesting collections. Look for your own initials.

ABOVE Even storage like these towering stacks of boxes could form the basis of a collection.

RIGHT A ring collection is displayed on a sculptural hand. The owner has also collected Indian tin boxes, which she has ingeniously turned into wall shelving.

FAR RIGHT A jewellery-maker has collected vintage photographs to provide her with inspiration.

the conventional choices are bookshelves and office shelving, but for an alternative display you could stack your books spines outward in colour-coded towers up and down a hallway.

Try to maintain the spirit of a collection in the way you display it. If you have gathered together fragile pieces – such as old perfume bottles, china figurines or dainty teacups, for example – keep them protected from inquisitive small fingers by storing them in Art Deco cabinets with lockable glass doors. If you have decided to hoard early editions of classic books, think about storing them in a complementary weathered-wood bookshelf from a similar period – or contrast their fine old looks by showing them off in a plastic modern modular shelving system.

Instead of hiding your beautiful serving dishes at the back of your kitchen cupboards, display them as they would have been in former times on wooden racks hung from the wall or on country-style sideboards with display shelves. Look for a Victorian tea trolley on which to show off your dainty teacups, saucers and teapots.

While many collections call for conventional display, think about how to arrange your treasured pieces in unusual places for maximum impact. Our eyes – like our ears – often fail to appreciate items that are presented to us in clichéd ways, so think about offbeat alternatives. If you have fallen for 1950s vases, for example, line the

whole lot up like soldiers along the centre of a table and crown them with big blooms. Or present your collection of old bottles by ranging them along a window ledge (the light will highlight the glass), and fill your disused fireplace with vintage vases. Eye-catching pieces demand eye-catching displays.

If you collect odd bits and bobs, you will need to store them – and you could create a subsidiary collection from the boxes you put them in. You might, for example, buy a series of small leather suitcases in which to store a collection of costume jewellery or old coins – or you could use a roll of vintage wallpaper to cover cardboard boxes of all shapes and sizes. Old gym lockers, which provide generous storage, sometimes surface at markets, while mail-sorting shelves or stacked wine boxes could be transformed into open pigeonholes that will allow you to savour your much-loved finds.

Putting it all TOGETHER

Plenty of fabrics, from the floral cushion covers to the large skin on the floor, soften the feel of this industrial-style London warehouse. From the Guy Rogers daybed to the nut-brown Chesterfield sofa, these pieces have been chosen for their classic good looks. Ethnic finds, such as the Moroccan pouffe and the little African table, add a note of eclectic chic.

Flea-market style is by its nature relaxing and comforting to live with because junk pieces with past lives are never precious, uptight or pretentious; they have been there, done that – and lived to tell the tale.

Relaxing Spaces

When trying to create a relaxing space in flea-market style, the big backdrops – the floors and walls – really count. If you want to include patterned furniture, keep your backdrops plain; paint or paper walls in a neutral shade and keep floors monochrome. If your living area is small, use optical illusions: light walls and floors will make the space look bigger, while dark canvases render a space smaller and more intimate. Mirrors always double the light in a room, so harness their powers. Choose one large mirror (such as a dressing-table mirror or full-length dressmaker's mirror) or create a mixture of styles by hanging a variety of mirrors on one wall.

If you like pattern but don't want to sacrifice a sense of space and openness, cover a single wall in vintage wallpaper, positioning plain furniture in front of it. Strips of wallpaper or textured wallpapers also create quirky backdrops. Consider stripped, stained or painted wooden floors. You can soften the look, and reduce noise, by throwing down textile finds such as old animal skins, including cowhides, goatskins and sheepskins, and rugs, such as Indian dhurries, Persian prayer mats and woven hearth rugs. Old carpets, which are frequently the first thing new owners strip out, also create foot-friendly floor covers. Simply cut them to the size you require.

ABOVE **If you are lucky, you may stumble across design classics such as this red Ercol sofa, adorned with a jewel-like collection of cushions. An ethnic rug provides warmth and softness underfoot.**

Your living room is one of the main public areas in the home, so it is worth taking time to style it entirely to your satisfaction. Most living rooms are organized around a single focal point such as a hearth, the home's traditional heartland. Seating often tends to be grouped around a low-level table (think kidney shaped 1950s tables, examples made from old railway sleepers and retro chrome and glass tables). Arrange your furniture in groups for conviviality, with sofas facing each other or armchairs set in a circle. If you don't like sitting shoulder to shoulder with

Signs of having been loved – a coffee-cup blemish on a table, a worn patch on an armrest, a slight indent on a sofa – make flea-market finds easy to accommodate.

others on a sofa, then assemble a collection of slouchy, inviting armchairs; it won't matter that they don't match, since they'll all share a laid-back vibe.

If your fireplace is meant to be a focal point, give it eye-catching style. Flea markets are often home to old accessories, including wrought-iron fireguards, coal scuttles, copper bellows, cinder brushes and pokers. The advent of the contemporary 'hole-in-the-wall' fireplace has been responsible for many new homeowners stripping out beautiful old fireplaces and mantelpieces. Restore the glamour of an old fireplace, but before lighting up have the chimney inspected and cleaned by a professional, and read up on the fuel-burning regulations in your area. Many urban areas require smokeless fuel or secondary burners for coal or wood fires to keep down pollution levels.

Lighting is the next priority. Living rooms need a combination of lights for different purposes. Apart from the vast choice of pendant lights on offer at markets, softer options include former office-desk lights for sofa-side reading and Victorian wall sconces for shining a wash of light on a wall, which has the bonus of making the room feel lighter and bigger. Everyone glows under the gentle light of a naked flame, so seek out vintage storm lanterns or candleholders of all shapes and sizes.

The most important buys for your relaxing room are the pieces of furniture. Finding a sofa that fits you and your style means that when you get home, you'll never want to move. It is worth emphasizing that you should always try out furniture before making a purchase. A sofa may look great, but when you sit on it you may find that its springs are shot or its frame is broken.

THIS PAGE Juxtapose pieces with a similar feel. In this living room, timeless classics, from the black leather Chesterfield sofa (whose ripped arm is covered by a throw) to the ornate side table, combine to create a refined, elegant look. In the absence of a sideboard, the drinks have been stashed in a large wooden wardrobe.

THIS PAGE **This sleek contemporary room is given a lived-in feel with found furniture. A chest of drawers, repainted white, provides storage, while a former desk offers a display surface for 1970s-style graphic vases.**

THIS PAGE This living room, with its to-die-for beige leather sofa, looks eclectic but elegant. Its canvases – the white walls and glossy black floor – make the perfect backdrop for a sculptural lamp, a cushion fashioned from a silk scarf and a portrait of the young Queen.

THIS PAGE **Create a haven for relaxation in an unexpected corner. In this guest bedroom, a chair upholstered in a soft, worn velvet cover makes an ideal place for repose. Peg rails, normally used in hallways, offer extra hanging space for visitors' coats and bags.**

If you like lying full length on the sofa to read or watch TV, make sure that whichever one you plan to purchase is the right size. And never judge a sofa by its cover. You can always use vintage fabric finds or dyed sheets, ex-army rugs and old curtains to re-upholster or re-cover an aged sofa. The repair process is not quite as simple in the case of leather sofas, since getting one of these re-upholstered can be as expensive as buying a new one. If black leather is ripped or worn, you could patch it up with tape; if the arm of your brown leather sofa has started to look worn, wrap it in a cover.

Many of us have already adopted and developed styles for our interior spaces based on trends of the moment. One very popular contemporary look combines old-world glamour with a minimalist twist, for example. Paint your floorboards and walls white, then choose a couple of stand-out pieces, such as a large, glossy brown leather sofa, an elaborate gilt mirror or one eye-catching pendant light, and soften the look with cushions made from luxurious second-hand fabric discoveries, including pashmina shawls, cashmere jerseys or even old silk dressing gowns.

ABOVE **Set against a backdrop of neutral floor and walls, this chintzy old sofa looks as good today as it did over 50 years ago.**

RIGHT Old leather club chairs sit comfortably side by side, flanking a classic lamp, originally designed for industrial use in the 1950s. Pieces like these are worth paying a little more for, particularly if they are in good condition, since they will retain their value.

BELOW A self-confessed lover of flea-markets, the owner of this apartment has based his seating arrangement on two good-quality sofas fashioned out of stiff, resilient calico. To protect their handsome visage, the sofas have been covered in thick blankets.

Use vintage fabric finds, old curtains or ex-army rugs to revive an old sofa.

Retro lovers will need to flip a few coins to choose between the wonderful range of sofas on offer. Low-level vinyl sofas or coloured leather sofas were once all the rage. When teamed with 1960s wooden sideboards or plastic modular storage, these pieces swing again in their original living-room setting. Complete the look with cushions in graphic prints and vintage rugs or cuts of 1960s and 1970s carpets.

When it comes to retro lighting, you can often find lamps that fit the appropriate colour scheme, such as, for example, plastic orange-shaded mushroom lights and large swooping floor chrome lights (similar to Castiglioni's 'Arco' lamp). Markets are often full of chunky 1950s and

THIS PAGE **This down-to-earth apartment in New York provides a perfect escape from the fast-pace of city life. One of its outstanding features is a pair of birdcages – a rarely spotted market find.**

ABOVE **This classic button-back sofa has been re-upholstered in thick, hard-wearing, former army blankets and accessorized with a Welsh blanket, a found cushion and a pillow covered with jute. Hanging on the wall behind the sofa is a quirky collection of plates and pictures that has gone to the dogs.**

graphic 1960s lamp bases as well as vases in which to show off flowers. Hang pot plants from the roof in macramé pot-plant holders.

Devotees of Modernist and Bauhaus pieces may also, if they are fortunate, uncover 20th-century classics with which to enliven their relaxing spaces. Finds of this kind can sometimes be valuable. Originals or close reproductions of classics such as an Eileen Gray 'Bibendum' chair, Arne Jacobson's 'Swan' chair, Verner Panton's plastic 'S' chair or Tom Dixon's 'Jack' light turn up from time to time on market stalls or car boots/yard sales. If you come across pieces of this kind in good condition, snap them up instantly because their value will only increase with time, while their looks remain timeless. More common pieces found

THIS PAGE This sofa has received a makeover in the form of a canvas cover. For a deconstructed look, seams are left on the outside. To create a clash of eras, an elaborate old frame borders a modern painting. Two empty picture frames have been given a career change, becoming lightshades.

LEFT A soft, dreamy light filtering through lace curtains gives this relaxing space an ethereal feel. Covering the generously large sofa is an old linen sheet, while a shawl is draped casually over its arm.

RIGHT A gorgeous modern rug has been fashioned out of a patchwork of cow hides. Propped up against the wall is a bestselling print of *The Chinese Girl* by Russian artist Vladimir Tretchikoff.

Soften a minimalist look with cushions covered in luxurious second-hand fabric finds, including silk dressing gowns, pashmina shawls or cashmere jerseys.

at markets include bent chrome and leather chairs. Soften modernist lines with cow hides on the floor or sew cushions out of zebra prints.

If you hanker after a country look, flea-market finds will fulfil your desires. Since your most expensive purchase is likely to be a sofa, buy one that optimizes the look, such as a large, squashy version covered with chintz, and pile it with tartan rugs and crocheted throws. If your discovery is the correct shape but needs new attire, clothe it in striped ticking fabrics or hardwearing canvas. Chairs to complete the look include old rocking chairs, wicker Lloyd Loom chairs, patio-style wooden chairs and benches made out of rustic woods.

If you need side tables for vases, coffee cups, books and lamps, look for school desks and outdoor furniture such as wrought-iron garden tables with

mosaic tops. Posies of wild flowers and bouquets of roses in odd found vessels such as bone-china tea cups, rustic French milk jugs and vintage bottles bring life and freshness to your space.

Relaxing spaces are not limited to living rooms. Other places of relaxation at home include nooks and crannies such as the end of a hallway, a space under the stairs or a large stair landing. Wherever it is quiet or where the sunlight falls is potentially a place to park. Flea markets offer up equally odd pieces on which you can recline, including colourful canvas hammocks, homemade swings, roll-out tatami mats and even blow-up Lilos. Since you are a flea-market shopper, you must be used to thinking outside the conventions of the matching three-piece suite, so seek out something original, something that will really help you to relax.

THIS PAGE AND OPPOSITE There is no need for preloved kitchen pieces to match. Second-hand finds will allow you to create an original space with timeless furnishings and accessories for next to nothing.

Flea market style will give a kitchen a cherished and lived-in feel. From big old biscuit tins to heavy coffee pots and huge cast-iron pans, preloved pieces add warmth to any kitchen.

Cooking and Eating Spaces

You could, if you wanted to, furnish your cooking and eating spaces almost entirely from flea markets, car boots/yard sales and online auctions – including the kitchen sink. One good reason for doing so is the sense of tradition that second-hand, vintage and preloved objects bring to these spaces. Most of us continue to cook and eat as we always have done, but time spent preparing meals has steadily diminished. While the generation of home cooks before us spent up to an hour each night preparing the family meal, our increasingly fast-paced lives have reduced this time to a matter of minutes.

But however long food takes to cook or prepare, most of us still love the rituals of dining – the solid feel of heavy flatware, the taste of water sipped from delicate tumblers and the bouquet of wine poured from a carafe into thin-stemmed, wide-bowled wine glasses. And we are still magnetized by the feel-good warmth of the long kitchen table.

Where cooking and eating rooms were customarily separate, in modern homes they are more often rolled into one big space in which the eating area combines with the food preparation area, farmhouse-style. And, while a kitchen

LEFT Mismatched chairs, retouched in pastel shades of eggshell paint, sit attentively at a long, thin table covered by a found yellow linen table runner. Dried hydrangea heads in former graveyard vases add to the faded, otherworldly beauty of this sun-filled eating space.

OPPOSITE This extensive collection of crockery, all found at a Brussels market and stacked according to the vessels' uses, colours or eras, is given a home in a huge built-in skyscraper of a shelf, reached by means of an extendable ladder.

table is generally used for food preparation and the communal breaking of bread, it is also a place where family members and friends gather for chat, homework, a glass of wine, games or other leisure activities.

When it comes to furnishing your cooking and dining space, the first thing you need to do is decide what kind of look you are hoping to achieve. If you have a sleek contemporary kitchen, you might want to add a handful of vintage treasures to bring it a sense of soul and individuality. Contemporary off-the-peg kitchens can look rather sterile and clinical, but older pieces lend them depth and character. And these slick, modern kitchens make clean-lined canvases against which you can show off your fabulous finds.

Modern doesn't have to mean buying new. For a modern classic look in the kitchen, keep the feel minimalist, hiding clutter behind smooth cupboard doors. Display finds such as one curvaceous retro-style vase with flowers on a mantelpiece and if you do show off your kitchenwares, ensure that they are space-enhancing (a shiny silver coffee pot or a chrome toaster, for example), classic (a silver hob kettle or a Victorian water jug) or elegant (second-hand champagne flutes or a curvaceous teapot).

Add depth to a contemporary eating space by adorning a polished new glass-topped table with one beautiful antique candelabrum. There's no need to buy new chairs when second-hand markets are absolutely overflowing with an array of classics ranging from Edwardian

THIS PAGE The centrepiece of this eating area is a 1950s conference table created for office use. Polished and adorned with a pair of old candelabra, it is now a stylish dining table.

OPPOSITE, ABOVE Many cooking, eating and relaxing spaces are now rolled into one large open-plan area. In this home a 1970s sofa bed mixes with an antique high chair, wooden café chairs and old copper pans.

mahogany sets, bent chrome and leather chairs, bentwood café chairs and moulded-plastic chairs. You can always fashion your own dinner table from a smooth, repainted door mounted on trestles or an old boardroom table.

If you want to clad a modern table in classic garb, look out for white linen and damask napery (matching tablecloths and napkins). Once given as wedding presents or passed down as family heirlooms, these beautiful sets, often monogrammed, make rare appearances at markets and antiques fairs. If you can't find a complete set, an ensemble of non-matching napery is easy to create and looks just as good. Crown your table with a glamorous centrepiece such as a stunning vase of flowers or a low-hanging, sparkling chandelier.

A country-style kitchen is particularly well suited to flea-market finds – right down to the kitchen sink (a ceramic butler's sink, of course). For the walls, consider tongue-and-groove cladding, terracotta tiles or vintage floral wallpaper. For storage, choose freestanding pieces such as painted cupboards and old plate racks. Fabrics are an integral part of the country look, so scour markets for traditional

BELOW The table is a market find that has been given a smart zinc top. On the table, a small blue cast-iron pot makes a funky vase.

BELOW RIGHT Revive cupboards by painting doors in a rainbow of colours and give them chi-chi handles, as seen here.

If you already have a sleek contemporary kitchen, you can adorn it with a handful of vintage flea-market finds to give it a little soul.

THIS PAGE The dining room in the same house combines contemporary classics with antique finds. On the boardroom-style chair is a cushion fashioned from a vintage Christian Dior scarf. On the 1970s table is an antique Indian pot with a single white flower.

THIS PAGE A pair of found bar stools transform a worktop into a breakfast bar. The antique silver flatware is a collection of single pieces, while the Moroccan tea glasses are a typical market find.

RIGHT A plain backdrop allows for a subtle play of pattern and colour. The 1970s table is covered with floral vintage bark cloth.

country patterns (think floral, paisley or gingham) and fashion these pieces into tablecloths, curtains, tea towels or aprons. Create under-sink storage with a colourful gingham or ticking curtain strung along a wire.

If you collect country-style kitchen accessories, make a display of them. Pieces of enamelware, old copper pots, wooden chopping boards, handmade pottery, patterned plates, old coffee grinders and big copper kettles need to be showcased from like-minded shelves and cupboards such as old bookshelves, wardrobes with no doors and old laundry racks fixed to the ceiling. Second-hand stoves and reconditioned ranges do occasionally turn up at markets or salvage yards, but it pays to have such major fixtures overhauled and installed by a professional. An old shallow butler's sink or deep Belfast sink teamed with brass taps is another way to embrace the country vibe.

For country-style eating spaces, start with a big table. Regional auction houses can be good hunting grounds. You may be lucky enough to find a large farmhouse or refectory table – or look for extendable pine tables or former boardroom tables to cover with a vintage tablecloth. For country-style seating, choose folding garden chairs, distressed painted chairs or an assortment of wooden chairs. Large benches, rather like big tables, bring people together, so look for old church pews or school benches to seat your dinner guests (soften hard edges with cushions covered in vintage fabrics).

If you long to create a retro look, you need to go no further than your local market or even charity shop/thrift store. You may be fortunate enough to unearth Formica-topped cupboards and sideboards from the 1950s. If not, many high-street stores sell good reproductions, which you

LEFT An old tin makes a beautiful container for a bouquet of amaryllis. This old farmhouse-style table and its accompanying quartet of ex-café chairs are all classic market finds.

LEFT An old tin makes a beautiful container for a bouquet of amaryllis. This old farmhouse-style table and its accompanying quartet of ex-café chairs are all classic market finds.

ABOVE Once used as a hunting table in France, this long narrow table makes a convivial dining spot. The old school chairs, made comfortable with cushions sewn from vintage floral fabrics, were cast-offs from a local coffee-shop.

OPPOSITE The crowning glory of this dining room is an exquisite chandelier, found in almost mint condition at a market. The antique mirror behind reflects its beauty.

can easily accessorize with finds such as colourful melamine plates, cups and bowls, graphically decorated or pastel-coloured tableware, retro toasters and hob kettles, and kidney-shaped fruit bowls and vases. For a 1950s look, choose pieces in pastel. If it's a 1960s vibe that you're after, go for strong, vibrant colours (red, yellow, purple) and psychedelic patterns.

Markets and car boots/yard sales can furnish any retro dining space. Scour stalls for pieces such as round plastic tables with matching moulded chairs, curvy wooden chairs, mid-century dining sets and oval wooden tables. For total authenticity with a dash of kitsch, serve drinks from a low-level wooden 1960s sideboard or wheel them in on a trolley. Cover your table with

tablecloths sewn from retro fabrics such as florals and candy stripes from the 1950s, graphic circles and swirls from the 1960s, or graphic fruit patterns from the 1970s.

Cooking and eating spaces are also able to accommodate an eclectic look that consists of mismatched but beautiful objects. The common denominator will, of course, be your taste. While an all-out eclectic look can work (modern alongside classic, high tech with old tech), you may find that your own style falls into a new genre. Many markets are full of goods and food ideas from around the world, including chinoiserie tea caddies, bamboo steamers, tagine dishes, jade chopsticks, large Japanese soup bowls, Indian thali dishes and old French preserving pans.

Use your eye – and your tastebuds – to create your own eclectic look. 'Global ethnic', for example, might be reflected in a very simple, utilitarian cooking space dressed with accessories such as Moroccan tea glasses and Ethiopian coffee pots, while the eating space is informal, focused on a low-level table, with colourful floor cushions strewn all around. To create a low table, simply saw the legs off a taller one; to make your own cushion collection, sew Indian saris into covers for cushions for your guests to sit on. Source goods from local ethnic markets as well as markets you come across

on your travels. Whatever your style, flea markets will give you the opportunity to indulge your penchant for forgotten eating fashions. Revive fads such as 1970s fondue parties, cake decorating, pressure-cooking, coffee mornings, or the rituals of old-fashioned afternoon tea. You can serve tea from bone-china cups and cake from a cake stand, find old lace doilies for plates and adorn your teapot with a knitted cosy.

When it comes to shaping your cooking and eating areas, be honest about your needs. If you really do cook and eat on the run, then pick flea-market finds to suit your

THIS PAGE AND OPPOSITE This kitchen is full of
otherworldly charm, its plain visage dressed up with
beautiful vintage things. Pieces of old wallpaper, antique
postcards and sepia-toned photographs are stuck with
masking tape to a perfectly ordinary fridge. The Belfast
sink, the metal dish rack and the bentwood chairs add
to its glamorous but careworn looks.

lifestyle as well as your style. If you live on your
own but like to host the odd dinner party, choose
flexible pieces, such as tables with drop leaves or
slide-away leaves and folding chairs. If you live
alone and eat out all the time, turn your back on
a big cook–eat space and go for a practical
breakfast-bar arrangement instead. Perch at a high
bench on spindly 1950s bar stools or sturdy old
laboratory stools. If TV dinners are your thing,
look for breakfast trays, large coffee tables and
low-level sofas so you can sit down, relax and feast
on your takeaway in second-hand style.

COOKING AND EATING SPACES 101

THIS PAGE To sleep, perchance to dream, in a room full of preloved finds. To soften the minimalist style of the bedroom, all the pieces of furniture are made from warm natural woods.

If you really can't decide exactly what style of bedroom you want, keep an open mind and let the pieces you find dictate the look.

Sleeping Spaces

Sleep the sleep of kings in your bedroom, and do it in second-hand style. While bedrooms are intimate spaces, they also say much about us as individuals – just walk into any bedroom and deduce from the style and state of the room what kind of person inhabits it. Market finds can help you express yourself in your bedroom. And, in a bedroom styled to reflect just who you are, you will sleep easily.

Picture this. In your room is a headboard constructed from a salvaged gate, a rickety garden chair bought from a village fair, and a cushion fashioned from a headscarf cherry-picked from a Paris flea market. Each individual item says so much about who you are and what you love. That's what makes your boudoir special.

When it comes to arranging and furnishing your bedroom, there are some tried-and-tested styles to choose from. To save time and money, try to keep in mind the overall style that you are attempting to achieve, since this will influence your purchasing decisions. And if you really can't decide on a style, maintain an open mind and let the pieces you find dictate the look.

If you strike it lucky at a French market, for example, you may discover a beautiful *lit bateau* bed hidden under dusty covers. With such an object as your room's centrepiece, you will naturally want to

Special finds make most impact when they strike an unexpected pose. Hang a patchwork quilt on a wall, for example, or turn it into a makeshift curtain.

ABOVE If you discover a beautiful bed frame but can't find a mattress to fit, do as this owner has done and insert a single divan within a queen-sized frame. The fabric on the bed and the valance are crafted from vintage fabrics, while the pillow is made from canvas sacking.

hunt down items to harmonize with its sophisticated style, such as a sparkling antique chandelier, vintage linen sheets, a silk kimono or an ornate chaise longue.

A minimalist style is popular in bedrooms because there is something quietly relaxing about pared-back lines and a lack of clutter. To keep the space simple, all you need is a few big and beautiful things. The rest of the room can be left bare. Start by making neutral backdrops of the floors and walls (strict minimalists keep to white or off-white), but try to avoid creating too much starkness; you can soften the look with plenty of fabrics, using pattern and colour

THIS PICTURE Crisp white cotton pillowcases offer a calm contrast to this ethnic quilt. On the wall, family photos are mounted on bulldog clips attached to tiny pins. A top hat is used as a desk tidy.

ABOVE Pale bedding and furnishings give this small bedroom a spacious, light and airy feel. The curtain and the valance are made from the same bolt of satin damask and add an unexpected note of glamour.

to magnetize the eye. One colourful silk cushion on a bed, for example, a large Turkish kilim on the floor or a white handmade lace shawl over the window is all you need to bring in warmth.

Unless you are lucky enough to have a separate dressing room, your bedroom will probably double as a dressing room. For lovers of minimalism, this means that efficient storage is vital. To create a streamlined space, you need to conceal your clothes and accessories in one enormous wardrobe, painted in simple colours or left in its natural garb. Oversized wardrobes/armoires – often crafted from beautiful old hardwoods such as oak, mahogany and cherry – turn up regularly at markets because many new owners banish these from their homes in favour of contemporary floor-to-ceiling fitted storage. When choosing a bed, look for a stunning piece with a plain or ornate white headboard.

THIS PAGE Why buy a wardrobe when you can hide your clothes behind curtains made from vintage fabrics? In this bedroom, other clothing items are stowed under the bed in deep wooden drawers painted in funky colours. The look here is East-meets-West, with traditional floral bedspreads teamed with oriental paper lampshades.

THIS PAGE The storage story continues. On an old strip of panelling fashioned into a shelf sit capacious bags found at an Indian market. Indian tins have been stuck onto the wall to provide quirky shelving for books and ornaments.

Dress the bed in light, airy, white neutrals, such as pure linen sheets. While intact antique linens can be found at many markets, you could also fashion your own minimal-style duvet covers out of a patchwork of white linen sheets.

There is something unpretentious and down-to-earth about country style's soft, faded look that is completely at home in bedrooms. A bedroom's star is always the bed, so choose from wrought-iron bedsteads, old hospital beds and wooden beds to work this look. Keep bed-frame paintwork in simple, honest white or leave it distressed.

When it comes to clothing your bed, there are a huge range of rustic choices, from floral duvet covers to crochet patchwork blankets and old eiderdowns with sateen covers. You can use eiderdowns as wall hangings or window covers if they are exceptional pieces. To revive an eiderdown, simply take it to the dry-cleaner or hang it out on a washing line in the sunlight for a day and follow up with a shake and a good vacuum.

Like big floral dresses and Wellington boots, patchwork has always been part of country-style interiors. To create your own works, study old patchwork quilts to see how many are sewn out of scraps of clothes such as floral dresses, silk scarves, tweed suit jackets, striped shirts and embroidered baby clothes. When creating your own masterpiece, scour vintage clothing markets for pieces like these, but also keep your eyes open for conventional soft-furnishing finds, such as striped cotton ticking, gingham tablecloths and floral bedspreads. Instead of duvet covers, you can clothe your bed with lovely old woollen blankets, such as tartan rugs and ex-army blankets. Country patterns – paisley, floral, stripes and ginghams – can also be used to make curtains, cushions and chair covers. If you want an abundance of pattern, remember to avoid visual overload by keeping the backdrop plain.

When it comes to storage, maintain the same themes by choosing distressed wardrobes, painted

ABOVE This plain door has been given a feminine twist with a layer of Anaglypta wallpaper. It's a fitting backdrop for a treasured piece of vintage finery.

RIGHT Every bed should be well dressed. While the trousers hanging over the end of the bed may be this year's Gucci, the beautiful cushions are yesteryear's silk scarves. Necklaces strung from the bedhead complete the outfit.

bookshelves and old wooden dressers. If you need alternative storage, use your country-style woven shopping bags, wicker hampers, tea chests and old suitcases. If you have room, consider acquiring an antique rocking chair, a wicker garden chair or a chocolate-brown leather armchair.

While bedrooms are designed for rest, they are also places for romance. Turn your room into a chic boudoir with pieces to please the senses. Create a come-hither space with tactile textures and seductive furnishings. Headboards are crucial to this look. Create your own by stretching a fake animal skin across a length of board or restore an old rococo-style headboard. Create an air of luxury with piles of pillows in an assortment of sizes and shapes. To complete the scene, put a classic piece of furniture alongside the bed, such as an old chaise longue or a Louis XVI-style armchair.

THIS PAGE **Two distinctive treasures – the ornate 1980s side lamp and the antique bedside cabinet – add a luxurious look to this pared-down loft bedroom.**

THIS PAGE Import preloved pieces into bedrooms to enhance character. In this room, a garden bench serves as a bedside table and an anglepoise desk light offers bedside illumination. A vintage tablecloth makes a chic alternative bedcover.

THIS PAGE A metal floral chandelier, a vintage scarf draped over a lamp, an angel cookie cutter, and an open fan are just a few of the disparate things that, strangely, look just right in this tranquil, lived-in bedroom. Plenty of white calms down the vibrant multi-pattern mix.

For a luxurious feel next to the skin, look for silk sheets at markets. For your bed cover, see if you can find velvet or velveteen curtains, popular in the 1980s, to fashion into oh-so-soft cushions or bedspreads. To complete this glamorous, sexy look, think lighting. Crown your room with one extravagantly large, low-hanging chandelier, or fit gothic wall sconces above the bed instead of bedside lights. Pleasure seekers will ensure that they get out of the right side of the bed each day by letting their feet step onto a sensuously soft rug – a fluffy sheepskin rug, for example.

If your style is more offbeat, seek out retro finds. Much of this particular quest is about discovering the right accessories, such as graphically decorated fabrics for bed covers, headboards, upholstery and cushions. Looks of the 1950s overlap a little with country style, which can be feminine at heart, especially if you go for the era's soft pastels – baby pinks, pea greens and lemon yellows – combined with chintzy florals and paisleys. For a 1960s vibe, mix graphic prints on soft furnishings derived from the vintage clothes, curtains and bedspreads. If pieces from the 1970s grab you, indulge your inner hippy

ABOVE **Groovy, baby. This 1970s bed, with its crazy car seat headboard, is flanked by lengths of vintage floral fabric to create the feel of an intimate four-poster in this airy warehouse.**

and find a kaftan to use as a dressing gown, dress your bed in a block-printed Indian cotton bedspread and spread a colourful dhurry on the floor.

For retro-style storage, scour markets and car boots/yard sales for low-level wooden sideboards. Instead of a conventional wardrobe, hang your clothes on a rolling rack and hide it behind one large piece of vintage fabric or an old curtain strung up from a wire. If you collect vintage clothes, then why hide them? Fit a selection of old brass hooks to a white-painted wall and use them to show off your prized pieces. Pile hats on a bentwood hat stand or use it to hold an array of vintage bags.

Alternatively, you can create your own look from flea-market discoveries by mixing and matching different styles and eras. Pieces used in unconventional ways – a side table crafted from a repainted kitchen stool, a fold-out garden chair covered in a lace scarf, an old school desk with the legs sawn

off – make eye-catching statements. Use an old sewing-machine trestle in place of a dressing table and find a Venetian-style mirror to lean against it.

Second-hand markets are full of handy storage items, including good-quality coat-hangers, proper wooden suit-hangers, jewellery trinket boxes, hatboxes, shoehorns, shoe racks, lavender bags and large wicker laundry baskets. You will find yourself lingering over stalls of beautiful, memory-evoking items from the past, such as old photographs, Chinese fans, pinned butterflies in box frames, oil paintings and vintage magazines. Any of these can be used to embellish your bedroom walls.

Once you have hunted down all the things that make you feel most at home, curl up and take a quick nap. After all, shopping is such hard work.

ABOVE LEFT A brightly coloured patchwork blanket from a baby's cot/crib adds visual interest to a white, minimalist bedroom. The curtain was made by sewing together strips of vintage floral and striped fabrics.

ABOVE RIGHT For a little luxury, track down an original kimono to swan around in, like the red one seen here. A delicate lace panel makes a pretty window shade.

THIS PAGE If you uncover an old metal bedframe like this, snap it up. Conceal any under-bed sins with a valance, which you can create from tablecloths or old bedspreads. To show off finds, create a gallery spacesuch as these built-in cupboards and shelves.

THIS PAGE **Bathrooms**
should be relaxing places,
devoted to the revival and
refreshment of body and
soul. From the gentle,
off-white colour scheme
to the flea market
accessories – a tin-saucer
soap dish, an ornate mirror
and a hand-made wooden
stool – everything in this
room is conducive to calm.

RIGHT Every bathroom needs a mirror, so, if you come across one whose shape you like but the frame is dull, all you need to do is to repaint it.

Bathrooms are intimate and sensual spaces – one of the few really private places in the home – so make them yours with things you love.

Bathing Spaces

Traditionally, bathrooms have been treated as something of an afterthought when it comes to the design and decoration of a home. Unlike kitchens and living rooms, they tend to be private, intimate spaces, often tucked away in small rooms. While bathrooms are primarily functional, we are now demanding that they should also be comfortable havens of peace, where we can soothe away all our cares.

That is where flea-market style comes in. The items that can be found at markets – large rolltop tubs, large Victorian shower-rose heads, antique mirrors – all look beautiful, extolling a timeless, lived-in look. And, while it is important to get your bathroom's practical elements right, the pieces you will pick up at markets, antiques

fairs, car boots/yard sales and even online auctions will help you to get the aesthetics right so that you can use your steamy sanctuary for genuine relaxation.

Start with the basics: the floors and walls. In many houses, the bathroom is located in the smallest, darkest room in the home. If this is true in your case, use optical illusions to make the space seem bigger. To 'create' space, you need to maximize the light in the room, so keep large surfaces glossy and the overall colour scheme light and bright.

The need for lightness extends to floors, which can be covered with reclaimed tiles or stripped wooden timbers. The shinier the floor, the more light it will reflect, so coat your timber in a glossy varnish. Linoleum, currently back in vogue, is one of those

THIS PAGE With its pink, blue and white colour scheme, this room is peaceful and reassuring. The candy-coloured woven-plastic chair is both attractive and waterproof. A magazine rack holds bathtime reading.

LEFT At the end of the day, nothing is more soothing than the soft, warm light of candles. These ones stand in old enamel lamplighters.

THIS PICTURE A glass-fronted cabinet repainted in a tranquil blue is filled with quirky, witty objects for the bather to admire. Its mirrored back reflects light around the room and enhances the feeling of space in the room.

ABOVE This crocheted rug and vintage vest are common market finds. Dirty laundry often ends up in bathrooms so tidy it into a container like the string bag seen here.

THIS PICTURE **Built-in bath surrounds don't have to be boring. This one has been given a facelift with vintage fabric that has been treated with waterproofing spray. As an alternative, use waterproof wallpaper or PVC tablecloths.**

floorings many people strip out of their new homes in favour of more contemporary floor coverings, but the good news is that lino is a hardwearing, splash-proof, child-friendly flooring. If you can't find enough to cover your floor, cut off a strip to use as a mat in areas prone to splashes and spills.

When you step out of your bathtub, you will want to step onto something that is kind to the soles of your feet. It is possible to find mats made from original duckboard slats, chenille towelling or natural cork. Alternatively, make a mat from a thick towel or a piece of carpet, or use a rug.

White tiles are hard to beat – they are functional and always look simple and chic. If you decide to opt for new tiles, keep your eyes open for off-beat second-hand examples to add interest to a too-smooth expanse of new tiling. For example, you could create a patchwork of old white-and-blue Delft tiles (often stripped out of Victorian bathrooms) or add a narrow strip of colourful Moroccan mosaic tiles. For a rustic feel, clad your walls in reclaimed wood from a salvage yard.

A bathroom wall's ornaments are its mirrors. While you need mirrors for daily bathroom rituals, you can also, by strategic positioning, use them to harness the spatial powers of light. If you find a mirror that's the right shape but has an unattractive frame, simply repaint the frame in a colour to suit your room or make one yourself out of natural objects such as found sea-shells, sand-coloured pebbles or driftwood. If you have limited wall space, you could give wall-mounted bathroom cabinets a shiny new mirrored face to help enhance the light.

The centrepiece of most bathrooms is, of course, the bathtub. One of the most popular fixtures, which brings with it an air of luxury and indulgence, is an antique cast-iron, claw-footed, rolltop tub. If you find a bathtub with chipped or cracked enamel it is possible to have it re-enamelled, but bear in mind that this can be

Give a new bath character with a cladding of vintage wallpaper, reclaimed timber or a patchwork of old tiles.

very expensive. Look for reconditioned taps/faucets and spout fittings, which should always be installed by a professional plumber. If you find a bathtub with broken legs, simply remount it on slats of antique reclaimed timber or even breeze blocks.

Even in a bathroom, flea-market style defies tradition. If the idea of a conventional matching three-piece suite doesn't appeal to your sense of style, your bathroom could be a happy mismatch of reclaimed bathtub, basin and lavatory. You could marry an old copper tub with a Victorian lavatory and a washstand backed with old tiles, or combine a rolltop tub with a Belfast sink and a 1930s lavatory with a reclaimed mahogany seat. For a bathroom with a sense of fun,

dress your lavatory in a kitsch, colourful towelling seat cover and paint the outside of the bath and the cupboard below the basin in contrasting colours.

If you have sufficient space, other pieces of furniture can be used to add to the feeling of repose, such as deep armchairs, chaise longues or daybeds. Apart from adding to the sense of comfort and luxury in the room, such seating makes it easier to carry out beauty routines such as pedicures and facials. A mahogany or faux bamboo towel rail or a hat rack for discarded clothes will always come in handy. Small tables, such as wrought-iron garden tables, provide ideal surfaces for stacks of towels, a vase of fresh flowers or lotions and potions.

ABOVE LEFT A gallery of mirrors in all shapes and sizes creates an eye-catching display to maximize light from the skylight above.

ABOVE RIGHT The initial 'E' and old postcards add a personal touch to a small bathroom. For an air freshener with a difference, drill holes into a block of wood and burn incense.

THIS PAGE This calm space is dominated by a large mirror and a picture of a nude with downcast eyes, both sitting alongside dishes, angular vases and an ornate glass candlestick on a wooden work bench.

OPPOSITE This room is full of beautiful finds: the 'tables' (wooden crates resting on their ends), the Belfast sink with old copper taps and the glamorous, necklace-draped mirror.

For total relaxation, the view from the bathtub needs to be uncluttered, so keep everything tidied away by installing ample storage. Old bathroom cabinets are easy to find at markets and reclamation yards and you can import other storage ideas from around the home. Pile towels into chests of drawers, and house your toiletries in old medical cabinets or an unused bedside drawer.

When it comes to small storage, market finds and their uses are infinite. You can, for example, use old pails or olive-oil cans as waste bins and put your toothbrushes in vintage vases or coloured-glass tumblers. Pile rolls of toilet paper in old shopping baskets or hatboxes and use sculptural ashtrays and delicate china saucers as soap dishes.

Old grooming items sometimes turn up at markets, including manicure sets, hand mirrors, eyelash curlers, bone-handled hairbrushes, curlers and shaver brushes. These implements are often sturdy and built to last, and do the job much better than their flimsy contemporary counterparts.

With all your clutter swept away, the next thing is to evoke a calm, peaceful atmosphere. A small posy of flowers in an old china tea cup or a leafy green plant in a Victorian chamber pot will give you something living and breathing to look at. You can also bring yourself back to earth with finds from nature, such as coral, shells, fossil swirls and pieces of sculptural driftwood.

The flickering, warm light of a flame is soft on tired eyes so, for an ultra-soothing effect, transform your bathroom at night into a grotto of candles. Place your candles in old storm lanterns, elegant oil lamps or graceful antique candelabra, or dot tealights in Moroccan tea glasses around the room.

To enhance your privacy, use beautiful window coverings to exclude prying eyes while maintaining an aesthetically pleasing look. To let light diffuse through the curtains, source pieces such as lace shawls and linen tablecloths, or create a patchwork curtain from old silk scarves in pale colours.

ABOVE **A shower alcove has been tiled with second-hand tiles and accessorized with vintage towels.**

OPPOSITE **A sauna-like feel has been created in this bathroom by the use of reclaimed wood.**

When it comes to decorating your child's bedroom, flea-market style says, 'Come on, let's play!' There's something about finding furniture for children's rooms that allows our inner child to have free rein.

Children's Spaces

Children's spaces are their studies and bedrooms – and, if you are lucky, a separate rumpus room too. In most cases, children's play areas spill into parents' living areas, so, to keep the rising tide of primary-coloured plastic toys at bay, good storage is vital. To keep your own living space looking sane, hunt for finds such tea chests, trunks, suitcases, wicker baskets and laundry baskets that will fit in with your décor.

In your child's bedroom, however, you can let your hair down. It is a good idea to keep walls and floors neutral as children grow up fast and their tastes change accordingly. Let today's favourite pictures and posters of cartoons, cute animals and pop stars blow in and out onto blank spaces. The overall feel should be a relaxed one since the bedroom is where a child unwinds. Children love lively, exuberant colour schemes, but temper loud colours or bold pattern with plenty of deep contrasts and gentle, harmonious tones.

When buying bedroom furniture, there are plenty of beds to pick from, including wrought-iron cots/cribs and moses baskets/bassinets. If you are buying one of these for a young baby, it is important to always buy a new mattress for reasons of hygiene.

Scour markets for small chests of drawers for a nursery or children's room; if you find a less than attractive version that's just the right size, you can always strip it and repaint it in your child's favourite colour. Children who are old enough to dress themselves will love having storage that is easy to access, so store their clothes and shoes at a low level in brightly coloured plastic shopping baskets or sturdy boxes covered in wallpaper remnants or gift wrap.

ABOVE If you find an old armchair in reasonable condition, customize it for a children's bedroom by re-upholstering it in colourful fabrics or sewing a loose cover. Take home waifs and strays like this floppy-eared bunny.

OPPOSITE This modern hospital-style cot has been spray-painted to give it a new lease of life. While the bright pop of colour is very effective, try to avoid colour overdrive. Remember that bedrooms are where your children unwind and relax. Use plenty of white space to strike a balance.

THIS PAGE **Create a patchwork of patterns on a bed.** Here striped pillow cases, floral pillow covers and chinoiserie-style sheets combine to make an eye-catching mélange.

OPPOSITE Irresistible eye-candy for a little girl, the wall behind the wardrobe is a collage of wallpaper scraps, collected from ends of rolls, pattern books and swatch samples.

A small wardrobe/armoire is always handy, but if your child likes choosing his or her own clothes, fasten a pole between two solid wooden posts nailed to the wall for open clothes storage.

For bedroom chairs, re-upholster or create covers for second-hand armchairs from colourful, sturdy vintage-textile finds such as canvas, ticking fabrics, former curtains and bedspreads. Or accessorize a plain armchair with brightly coloured cushion covers adapted from vintage fabrics such as old scarves, aprons and dresses.

Cover your child's bed in colourful finds such as crocheted rugs or patchwork duvets, or dye plain cot blankets. Making a patchwork bedcover for an adult's bed is daunting, but creating a patchwork throw from vintage finds for a baby's cot is less of a challenge; you can always add on bits as your baby moves from bassinet to cot/crib to single bed. Old children's clothes, particularly those incorporating embroidery, lacework or prints, are an ideal starting point for a patchwork cover. One natural fabric that is gentle on young children's skin is linen. If you find antique linen sheets, simply cut them up to cot sizes and dye them.

Good storage in children's bedrooms is essential, especially if your child is a natural magpie. Most children also like to see their possessions out on

OPPOSITE **Hand-me-downs** like these children's chairs often end up in markets when they get to the end of the line; in this case, all that was needed was a new coat of paint. Children like things with a sense of fun, such as the blow-up beach balls and globes hung from the ceiling. Look out for mural-sized artworks like this Russian scene, which absorb children for hours.

RIGHT Take some of the work out of homework by giving your children a bright and sunny place to study. In this room, a 1970s-style storage system is used to tidy away pens, pencils, rulers and other stationery. For a study light, a rusty anglepoise lamp has been sprayed with cherry-red gloss paint, and an old typist's chair has been repainted buttery yellow.

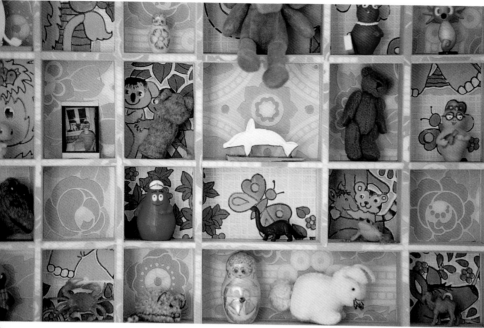

ABOVE Open shelving has been transformed into a zoo for stuffed animals. Lined in old pieces of wrapping paper and scraps of vintage wallpaper, it is a visual feast for tiny eyes.

Children love bright colour schemes, but temper loud colours with gentle, harmonious tones.

ABOVE Old coat hooks,, make an open showcase for a vintage hand-knitted child's coat displayed on a crocheted coat hanger.

ABOVE An ordinary chest of drawers looks pretty in its new pink coat. The elephant on top is made out of a vintage towel; the gaudy ornament beside it has become a flower pot.

display, so try to combine open storage with chests, boxes or suitcases. For open shelving, reuse old bookshelves.

No matter how hard you try to resist, you will find that you often go to a market with your own shopping list and return with a collection of orphaned toys. Second-hand finds cost far less than shop-bought ones and, given the fickleness of children's affections, buying from markets means that you won't have spent a fortune on something that lasts only for five minutes.

While markets offer plenty of yesterday's toys – old tin soldiers, stuffed animals, rocking horses and Russian dolls – you will also find a huge array of grown-up playthings and knick-knacks that children adore: old trinket boxes, garden gnomes, sea shells, cowboy hats, garlands – you name it. If you are brave, take your child along with you to a second-hand market and see it from their perspective. If you get them to enjoy shopping from markets at an early age, they'll love it for life.

THIS PAGE **Instead of a conventional chest of drawers, reclaim an old desk and paint it a vibrant colour. The beautiful vintage Danish wooden cot is clothed in vintage fabric cushions and patchwork and woollen blankets.**

While some simply need a space to study, write letters and pay bills, for more and more of us the home office is our workplace.

Work Spaces

Tailor-made second-hand items for work spaces at home generally come from their original habitats: offices. Some pieces do turn up at markets, but office liquidation sales, office furniture auctions and second-hand office furniture outlets are often more fruitful picking grounds.

Office desks, available in various configurations, are ideal for the job for which they were designed. If a desk is too corporate in appearance, give it a makeover with a colourful coat of paint or hide it under an old tablecloth. If the desk has drawers, consider painting each drawer a different colour or giving the drawers a new set of knobs.

Early examples of desks, such as large rolltop desks, often come with plenty of built-in storage. Sometimes 'working' tables, built for long hours of labour – architects' drawing boards, leather-and-fabric cutting tables, factory assembly tables and antique sewing-machine trestles (sans machine) – turn up at markets when warehouses are stripped out, but tables that are more commonly found,

such as old school desks, small pine dining tables and glass-topped tables, work equally well.

Another solution is to make your own. For a cheap chic desk, rest a plain door on two support pillars such as towers of bricks, wooden trestles, bedside drawers or a duo of filing cabinets.

A good chair is essential. If you will be spending a lot of time at your desk, choose one that gives you adequate support. Try your chair before you buy it and remember the rules: your feet should be firmly planted on the floor (if they don't reach, a foot rest of second-hand books or an old winebox will do); your lower back must be well supported; and your arms must be at right angles to the desktop. Consider acquiring a typist's chair, which will be fully adjustable and ergonomically designed to support your posture. Give your chair a new personality by re-upholstering the seat and backrest in funky vintage-fabric finds.

Other chairs, such as leather boardroom chairs, architects' stools, school chairs and simple wooden

LEFT Former industrial pieces – such as the low-hanging factory lights, the long factory table (with its gorgeous customized legs) and the wall of filing cabinets – suit a former industrial space. Around the table is a collection of ex-office seats and factory chairs with swivel bases.

ABOVE Metal cabinets can be easily painted or stripped, but an original colour like this looks just right in this industrial-style room with its backdrop of painted brickwork. Pens, rulers and paintbrushes are stored on top of the cabinet in vases, tin cups, old mugs and bottles.

THIS PAGE There are many ways to fashion a desk. Here, old wooden trestles are crowned with a shiny new glass top. Instead of cushions to soften the seat of a chair, use a folded rug.

THIS PAGE Industrial-look discoveries are brought together to create a hard-working work station. Factory finds such as the desk, chair and metal shelving unit often surface at markets. On the desk is the perfect task light: a draughtsman's lamp.

chairs will also serve your desk well. If you need to adjust a chair to your height, shorten its legs with a saw or put a squab on the seat.

Every work space needs a light designed with reading in mind, and there is nothing to beat the adjustable anglepoise desk light (but check the joints and springs to ensure they are not too stiff or loose). Small bedside reading lamps or large floor lamps also throw out plenty of light.

In addition to office storage, most of us require some kind of filing system for keeping papers in order. Office furniture will do the job well, but may need customizing to fit in with a particular room's décor. Other storage ideas include old sorting office pigeonholes, chests of drawers, old metal gym lockers, old bookshelves and, for files, plate racks nailed to walls.

To keep your desk tidy, unearth something to suit your second-hand style rather than the ubiquitous plastic desk tidy. Store your pens, pencils, rulers and scissors in vintage vases, milk jugs, old tins, tea caddies, glass jars – whatever you can find. Builders' plastic odds-'n'-ends boxes – normally reserved for nails and screws – are ideal for staples, paperclips, erasers and sharpeners.

Markets and junk shops often reveal other early examples of desk accessories, including old Bakelite phones, quills and inkpots, kitsch paperweights, antique typewriters and bone-handled paper knives.

For storing notepads, staplers, hole-punchers and CDs, buy larger containers such as antique leather suitcases, jewellery chests, and hatboxes or cardboard shoeboxes jazzed up with vintage wallpaper or wrapping paper.

ABOVE **This tiny work space is shoehorned into the corner of a living room An old postal sorting cabinet provides plenty of storage for paperwork.**

RIGHT **You can find a work niche like this one in dead space beside or under the stairs. Here an industrial light is attached to the side of the staircase, illuminating a former printing-factory desk.**

OPPOSITE **This work corner, screened off with a patchwork of silk scarves, is home to a handsome old rolltop desk.**

Sources

Whether you're just browsing with the family, or simply a die-hard flea market freak, there are plenty of shopping opportunities both at home and away. Visit both in person and online. To find physical hunting grounds, look in local newspapers and on noticeboards for good old-fashioned jumble sales and car-boot sales. Smaller local markets often have bric-à-brac stalls, as do church, village, and school fetes. Visit local antique markets, charity shops/thrift stores, and architectural salvage and reclamation yards. Look out for auctions and keep an eye on skips/dumpsters and garage sales in your neighbourhood. In France, search for the nearest 'brocantes' – usually housed in a church or village hall. For larger antique and collector's markets, and European and American flea markets, go online to check dates, sites and sizes. America also excels in the 'sidewalk sale' or 'yard sale' – a sort of 'car boot from home' experience.

IN THE UK

LONDON MARKETS

My favourite website is *www.ilovemarkets.com* for the simple diary and up-to-date information about regular and one-off events in the city. Subscribe for useful market updates. Another good market location source is *www.streetsensation.co.uk*, a handy general guide to London's shopping streets. Click on through to the dedicated market streets section.

Spitalfields Market

Brushfield Street
London E1 6AA
www.oldspitalfieldsmarket.com
Visit the dedicated antiques market on a Thursday – it's a good one!

Portobello Market

Portobello Road
London W11
www.portobelloroad.co.uk
Friday and Saturday 8am–5pm
Head for the Golborne Road end – my favourite area.

Brick Lane Market

Brick Lane, Cheshire Street and Sclater Street
London E1 6SB
Sunday 8am–2pm
www.visitbricklane.org

Greenwich Market

Greenwich Church Street, Stockwell Street and Greenwich High Road, London SE10 9HZ
Saturday and Sunday 10am–5.30pm
www.greenwich-market.co.uk

MARKETS OUTSIDE LONDON

Regular organized antique markets and fairs around the UK are often located on airfields or racecourses. My favourite sites include Newark and Ardingly (*www.iacf.co.uk*) and Goodwood (*www.antiques-atlas.com*). Sunbury Antiques Market isn't far from London and is also very good (*www.sunburyantiques.com*). Larger fairs often span a long weekend/bank holiday, so if you're on a serious shopping trip it's advisable to allow two days to browse and buy. Many markets have a trade day – the entry fee may be a little more, but your booty could well be worth it. Aim to arrive early – there's often a queue where a bargain is to be found. Travelling on foot? Invest in a large, comfortable backpack with padded straps and fill it with durable canvas shoulder bags. That way you can collect while you browse. Rooms to fully furnish? Consider hiring a van as it may work out cheaper and more convenient than staggered deliveries.

IN EUROPE AND THE USA

For general information on dates and locations for antiques and flea markets in Europe and the USA, have a look at *www.fleamarket.com*. Another interesting site where you can pick up a few flea market tips is *www.fleamarketinsiders.com*. And you can search for a local listed US market at *www.myfleamarketguide.com*.

IN EUROPE

Research online in advance and ask local people and hotels and guest houses for the best places to head. Many markets are very well organized with permanent stalls, small shops and restaurants, and offer comprehensive guides and maps. Road markets often pitch stall after stall as far as the eye can see.

FRANCE

In Paris, I like to head to **Puces de Clignancourt** at Rue des Entrepots, Saint Ouen, 75018 Paris, Saturday, Sunday and Monday (*www.parispuces.com*) and **Puces de Montreuil** at Avenue de la Porte de Montreuil, 75020 Paris. Saturday, Sunday and Monday. Visit *www.brocantesfrance.com* for details of markets located outside the capital.

BELGIUM

www.belgiumtheplaceto.be has a good section on market shopping.

DENMARK

www.markedskalenderen.dk is a comprehensive market calendar covering second-hand markets all over Denmark.

THE NETHERLANDS

The Dutch are big market fans and *www.vlooienmarktenkalender.nl* lists most markets nationwide. I like to visit for

King's Day, the national holiday during late April, when entire towns and cities transform into one huge flea market. An event not to be missed!

IN THE USA

Here are a few of the larger US flea markets:
Brooklyn Flea, New York (*www. brooklynflea.com*);
Alameda Flea Market, San Francisco (*www.alamedapointantiquesfaire.com*);
Rose Bowl Flea Market, Pasadena (*www. rgcshows.com*);
The Raleigh Flea Market, Raleigh, NC (*www.raleighfleamarket.net*);

Daytona Flea & Farmers Market, Florida (*www.daytonafleamarket.com*);
Brimfield, Massachusetts (*www. brimfieldshow.com*);
Shipshewana Auction & Flea Market, Northern Indiana (*www. shipshewanatradingplace.com*);
First Monday Trade Days, Canton, Texas (*www.firstmondaycanton.com*);
Springfield Antique Show & Flea Market, Ohio (*www. springfieldantiqueshow.com*);
Austin Country Flea Market, Texas (*www.austincountry.citymax.com*);

ON THE WEB

Our virtual hunting ground, the incredible internet, provides access to an ever-growing wealth of online auctions, antiques and vintage shopping sites, enabling global shopping and a pool of unusual items – well worth a regular surf! I can hunt and trawl from site to site for hours, but always find myself returning to the following:
www.salvoweb.com
www.vntg.com
www.etsy.com
www.ebay.com

Picture Credits

All photography by Debi Treloar.

key a=above, b=below, r=right, l=left, c=centre.

Endpapers Story; **page 1** The Norfolk home of designer Petra Boase and family; **2** Designer Susanne Rutzou's home in Copenhagen; **3** Debi Treloar's home in London; **4** The home in Paris of Sigolène Prébois of Tsé & Tsé Associées; **5** The home in Paris of designer Catherine Lévy of Tsé & Tsé Associées and Dorette; **12-13** The London home of author, stylist and shop owner Emily Chalmers of Caravan Style and director Chris Richmond; **14** Owner of Crème de la Crème à la Edgar, Helle Høgsbro Krag's home in Copenhagen; **15 inset** Debi Treloar's home in London; **16a** Martin Barrell and Amanda Sellers' home in London; **16bl** Debi Treloar's home in London; **16br** The home in Copenhagen of producer and creative director Samina Langholz; **17** Debi Treloar's home in London; **18 & 19r** Martin Barrell and Amanda Sellers' home in London; **19l** Designer Susanne Rutzou's home in Copenhagen; **20b** The home in Paris of Sigolène Prébois of Tsé & Tsé Associées; **20a** The Philadelphia home of Glen Senk and Keith Johnson; **21** Anita Calero; **22-23** Designer Susanne Rutzou's home in Copenhagen; **24al** The Philadelphia home of creative directors Kristin Norris and Trevor Lunn; **24bl** The home in Paris of designer Catherine Lévy of Tsé & Tsé Associées and Dorette; **24r & 25** owner of Crème de la Crème à la Edgar, Helle Høgsbro Krag's home in Copenhagen; **26** Debi Treloar's home in London; **27 background** The Chestnut Hill home of Pamela Falk; **27 inset** The Norfolk home of designer Petra Boase and family; **28** Martin Barrell and Amanda Sellers' home in London; **28 inset** Debi Treloar's home in London; **29, 30 & 31l** The London home of author, stylist and shop owner Emily Chalmers of Caravan Style and director Chris Richmond; **31r** Debi Treloar's home in London; **32al** Designer Susanne Rutzou's home in Copenhagen; **32ar** The Philadelphia home of creative directors Kristin Norris and Trevor Lunn; **32b** The Philadelphia home of Glen Senk and Keith Johnson; **33l** Designer Susanne Rutzou's home in Copenhagen; **33r** Story; **34 both** The Norfolk home of designer Petra Boase and family; **35-36** Debi Treloar's home in London; **37l** The home in Copenhagen of producer and creative director Samina Langholz; **37r both** The Norfolk home of designer Petra Boase and family; **38-39** Designer Susanne Rutzou's home in Copenhagen; **38 inset** The Philadelphia home of Glen Senk and Keith Johnson; **39ar** The home in Copenhagen of producer and creative director Samina Langholz; **40** The guesthouse of the interior designer and artist Philippe Guilmin, Brussels; **40 inset & 41** Owner of Crème de la Crème à la Edgar, Helle Høgsbro Krag's home in Copenhagen; **42** The home in Copenhagen of producer and creative director Samina Langholz; **43** The guesthouse of the interior designer and artist Philippe Guilmin, Brussels; **44** Martin Barrell and Amanda Sellers' home in London; **45bl & ar** Designer Susanne Rutzou's home in Copenhagen; **45c** Owner of Crème de la Crème à la Edgar, Helle Høgsbro Krag's home in Copenhagen; **46** The home in Copenhagen of producer and creative director Samina Langholz; **47br** Designer Susanne Rutzou's home in Copenhagen; **47ar** Owner of Crème de la Crème à la Edgar, Helle Høgsbro Krag's home in Copenhagen; **48al** The home in Copenhagen of producer and creative director Samina Langholz; **48bl**, **48ar** & **49** The guesthouse of interior designer and artist Philippe Guilmin, Brussels; **50** The London home of author, stylist and shop owner Emily Chalmers of Caravan Style and director Chris Richmond; **51l** Debi Treloar's home in London; **51r both** The home in Paris of designer Catherine Lévy of Tsé & Tsé Associées and Dorette; **52** & **53 inset** The Chestnut Hill home of Pamela Falk; **54** & **55 main** The guesthouse of interior designer and artist Philippe Guilmin, Brussels; **55 inset** Designer Steven Shailer's apartment in New York City; **56 main** The home in Paris of designer Catherine Lévy of Tsé & Tsé Associées and Dorette; **56 inset** The Norfolk home of designer Petra Boase and family; **57l** Debi Treloar's home in London; **57r** The home in Copenhagen of producer and creative director Samina Langholz; **58l** Martin Barrell and Amanda Sellers' home in London; **58r** Debi Treloar's home in London; **59** The home in Paris of Sigolène Prébois of Tsé & Tsé Associées; **60** John Derian's apartment in New York; **61ar** Anita Calero; **61al** The home in Paris of designer Catherine Lévy of Tsé & Tsé Associées and Dorette; **61br** The home in Copenhagen of producer and creative director Samina Langholz; **62al** The Philadelphia home of Glen Senk and Keith Johnson; **62bl** owner of Crème de la Crème à la Edgar, Helle Høgsbro Krag's home in Copenhagen; **62ar** John Derian's apartment in New York; **62br** The Chestnut Hill home of Pamela Falk; **63l** The Philadelphia home of Glen Senk and Keith Johnson; **63r** Designer Steven Shailer's apartment in New York City; **64 all** Designer Susanne Rutzou's home in Copenhagen; **65 inset** Anita Calero; **65 main** Designer Susanne Rutzou's home in Copenhagen; **66al** & **br** The home in Paris of designer Catherine Lévy of Tsé & Tsé Associées and Dorette; **66ar** & **67** The London home of author, stylist and shop owner Emily Chalmers of Caravan Style and director Chris Richmond; **68-69 all** Story except **68ar inset** Martin Barrell and Amanda Sellers' home in London; **70-71 all** The home in Paris of designer Catherine Lévy of Tsé & Tsé Associées and Dorette except **70ar** The Philadelphia home of creative directors Kristin Norris and Trevor Lunn; **72-73** The home in Copenhagen of producer and creative director Samina Langholz; **74-75** The London home of author, stylist and shop owner Emily Chalmers of Caravan Style and director Chris Richmond; **76-77** The home in Copenhagen of producer and creative director Samina Langholz; **78** Designer Susanne Rutzou's home in Copenhagen; **79** Martin Barrell and Amanda Sellers' home in London; **80** The guesthouse of interior designer and artist Philippe Guilmin, Brussels; **81** owner of Crème de la Crème à la Edgar, Helle Høgsbro Krag's home in Copenhagen; **82b** John Derian's apartment in New York; **82a** Designer Steven Shailer's apartment in New York City; **83** Anita Calero; **84** The Philadelphia home of Glen Senk and Keith Johnson; **85** The Philadelphia home of creative directors Kristin Norris and Trevor Lunn; **86** Story; **87** Debi Treloar's home in London; **88-89** The home in Paris of designer Catherine Lévy of Tsé & Tsé Associées and Dorette; **90-91** The guesthouse of interior designer and artist Philippe Guilmin, Brussels; **92** The Philadelphia home of creative directors Kristin Norris and Trevor Lunn; **93 all** The home in Paris of Sigolène Prébois of Tsé & Tsé Associées; **94-95** Martin Barrell and Amanda Sellers' home in London; **96-97** Debi Treloar's home in London; **98** John Derian's apartment in New York; **98-99** The London home of author, stylist and shop owner Emily Chalmers of Caravan Style and director Chris Richmond; **99** owner of Crème de la Crème à la Edgar, Helle Høgsbro Krag's home in Copenhagen; **100-101 all** Story; **102-103** Designer Susanne Rutzou's home in Copenhagen; **104l** The Philadelphia home of Glen Senk and Keith Johnson; **104-105** The Chestnut Hill home of Pamela Falk; **105** John Derian's apartment in New York; **106-107** The home in Paris of designer Catherine Lévy of Tsé & Tsé Associées and Dorette; **108-109** Martin Barrell and Amanda Sellers' home in London; **110** owner of Crème de la Crème à la Edgar, Helle Høgsbro Krag's home in Copenhagen; **111** The guesthouse of interior designer and artist Philippe Guilmin, Brussels; **112** The Norfolk home of designer Petra Boase and family; **113** The London home of author, stylist and shop owner Emily Chalmers of Caravan Style and director Chris Richmond; **114r** The home in Copenhagen of producer and creative director Samina Langholz; **114l**, **115** & **116** Debi Treloar's home in London; **117-119** The Norfolk home of designer Petra Boase and family; **120** & **121r** The London home of author, stylist and shop owner Emily Chalmers of Caravan Style and director Chris Richmond; **121l** The home in Paris of Sigolène Prébois of Tsé & Tsé Associées; **122** The guesthouse of interior designer and artist Philippe Guilmin, Brussels; **123** Story; **124-125** The guesthouse of interior designer and artist Philippe Guilmin, Brussels; **126** The home in Paris of Sigolène Prébois of Tsé & Tsé Associées; **127** The Norfolk home of designer Petra Boase and family; **128-129** Debi Treloar's home in London; **130** The home in Paris of Sigolène Prébois of Tsé & Tsé Associées; **131-133** Owner of Crème de la Crème à la Edgar, Helle Høgsbro Krag's home in Copenhagen; **134-135** The guesthouse of interior designer and artist Philippe Guilmin, Brussels; **136** John Derian's apartment in New York; **137** The Philadelphia home of Glen Senk and Keith Johnson; **138** The London home of author, stylist and shop owner Emily Chalmers of Caravan Style and director Chris Richmond; **139b** The home in Paris of Sigolène Prébois of Tsé & Tsé Associées; **139a** Designer Steven Shailer's apartment in New York City.

Business Credits

Andrea Brugi
Samina Langholz, producer and creative director
www.andreabrugi.com
Pages 16r, 37l, 39ar, 42, 46, 48al, 57r, 61br, 72-73, 76-77, 114r.

Anita Calero Photography
www.anitacalero.com
Pages 21, 61ar, 65 inset, 83.

Anthropologie
A curated mix of clothing, accessories, gifts and home décor
www.anthropologie.com
Glen Senk and Keith Johnson
Pages 20a, 24al, 32ar, 32b, 38 inset, 62al, 63l, 70ar, 84, 85, 92, 104l, 137.

Barrell & Sellers
Martin Barrell and Amanda Sellers
www.barrellandsellers.co.uk
Pages 16a, 18, 19r, 28, 44, 58l, 68ar, 79, 94-95, 108-109.

Bois-Renard
Pamela Falk's decorative home accessories
Pages 27 background, 52, 53 inset, 62br, 104-105.

Crème de la Crème à la Edgar
Childrens' clothing and accessories
Helle Høgsbro Krag, designer
www.cremedelacremealaedgar.com
Pages 14, 24r, 25, 40 inset, 41 , 45c, 47ar, 62bl, 81, 99, 110, 131-33.

Debi Treloar
Photographer and location owner
www.debitreloar.com
Pages 3, 15 inset, 16bl, 17, 26, 28 inset, 31r, 35-36, 51l, 57l, 58r, 87, 96-97, 114l, 115, 116, 128-29.

Dorette
Catherine Lévy, artist and jewellery designer
www.dorette.fr
Pages 5, 24bl, 51r both, 56 main, 61a, 66al & br, 70-71 all, 88-89, 106-107

Emily Chalmers
Interior stylist, author and shop owner
www.emilychalmers.com
www.caravanstyle.com
Pages 12-13, 29, 30, 31l, 50, 66ar, 67, 74-75, 98-99, 113, 120, 121r, 138.

John Derian Company Inc.
Designer and shop-owner
www.johnderian.com
Pages 60, 62ar, 82b, 98, 105, 136.

Petra Boase
Illustrator and designer
www.petraboase.com
The Norfolk home of Petra Boase
Pages 1, 27 inset, 34 both, 37r, 56 inset, 112, 117-19, 127.

Philippe Guilmin
Interior designer and artist; proprietor of boutique B&B
"Chambres en Ville"
Pages 40, 43, 48bl, 48ar, 49, 54, 55 main, 80, 90-91, 111, 122, 124-25, 134-35.

Rützou A/S
Susanne Rutzou, fashion designer
www.rutzou.com
Pages 2, 19l, 22-23, 32al, 33l, 38-39, 45bl, 45ar, 47br, 64, 65 main, 78, 103.

Sigolène Prébois, designer
www.tse-tse.com
Pages 4, 20b, 59, 93 all, 121l, 126, 130, 139b.

Steven Shailer
Pages 55 inset, 63r, 82a, 139a.

Story
An ever-changing and evolving lifestyle gallery/shop/deli
owned by stylist Ann Shore
www.storydeli.com
Endpapers, pages 33r, 68-69 (all except 68ar), 86, 100-101, 123.

Tsé & Tsé Associées
Modern French design, founded in 1991 by Sigolène Prébois
and Catherine Lévy
www.tse-tse.com
Pages 4, 5, 20b, 24bl, 51r, 56 main, 59, 61a, 66al, 66br, 70-71, 88-89, 93, 106-107, 121l, 126, 130, 139b.

Index

Page numbers in *italics* refer to illustrations

Acknowledgments

Emily Chalmers would like to thank everyone who made this book possible, especially Alison Starling, for dreaming up the wonderful project; Gabriella Le Grazie, for getting in touch and directing us in her special way; Emily Westlake, for her support; Paul Tilby, for his graphics skills; and Henrietta Heald and all the hard-working team at Ryland Peters & Small. Ali, thank you once again for your optimism and inspiration; and thank you to all those flea-market fans who allowed us to feature their wonderful homes.

A special thank you goes to the lovely Debi Treloar – my flea-market friend.

Ali Hanan's thanks goes to Henrietta Heald for her thoughtful, sensitive editing; to Alison Starling for asking her to work on such a lovely book; to the vivacious, warm and wonderful Emily Chalmers for her flowers, conversation and inspirational ideas; and to her own in-house team, Dizzy, Luca and tiny Rosa.